NEXT MOVES

To Glenn A. Kent, colleague and teacher

NEXT MOVES
An Arms Control Agenda for the 1990s

§

Edward L. Warner III
David A. Ochmanek

Council on Foreign Relations
New York

COUNCIL ON FOREIGN RELATIONS BOOKS

The Council on Foreign Relations, Inc., is a nonprofit and nonpartisan organization devoted to promoting improved understanding of international affairs through the free exchange of ideas. The Council does not take any position on questions of foreign policy and has no affiliation with, and receives no funding from, the United States government.

From time to time, books and monographs written by members of the Council's research staff or visiting fellows, or commissioned by the Council, or written by an independent author with critical review contributed by a Council study or working group are published with the designation "Council on Foreign Relations Book." Any book or monograph bearing that designation is, in the judgment of the Committee on Studies of the Council's board of directors, a responsible treatment of a significant international topic worthy of presentation to the public. All statements of fact and expressions of opinion contained in Council books are, however, the sole responsibility of the author.

Library of Congress Cataloging-in-Publication Data

Warner, Edward L.
        Next moves : an arms control agenda for the 1990s / Edward L. Warner III, David A. Ochmanek.
        p. cm.
        Includes index.
        ISBN 0-87609-049-8
        1. Arms control. I. Ochmanek, David A. II . Council on Foreign Relations. III. Title.
        JX1974.W26 1988
        327.1'74--dc19   88-37894
                                                                       CIP

CONTENTS

FIGURES

TABLES

Foreword

The incoming Administration will be faced with a variety of arms control issues, each of which is connected with corresponding issues of force structure and force balance, international relations (especially between the U.S. and the U.S.S.R.) and domestic politics. Strategic offensive and defensive arms negotiations are the furthest along, but the conventional balance in Europe increases in military importance and in political significance as nuclear forces are limited, reduced, or rhetorically devalued. Other issues include tactical nuclear weapons, chemical warfare, nuclear testing and antisatellite weapons. To assist in outlining the arms control agenda and suggesting some of the factors that future U.S. positions will have to take into account, the Council on Foreign Relations convened a study, organized by Michael Mandelbaum of the Council staff, on "The Next Administration's Arms Control Agenda."

Four meetings, which I chaired, were held during the period from January through May of 1988. A group of fifteen to twenty Council members and others, changing somewhat from meeting to meeting, commented on and debated papers on the arms control legacy of the Reagan administration, Gorbachev and arms control, strategic defenses, and conventional arms control. In each case the discussion dealt as well with the military balance and with related political issues.

The range of viewpoints of the participants was significant but not extraordinary; still, Frank Gaffney and Brian Hehir found much on which to differ. The authors of the present volume, Messrs Ochmanek and Warner, thus had a chance to hear varied comments on the issues before deciding how they would treat those issues.

Several factors make it likely that there will be further arms control agreements during the next four years. One is the new style and altered priorities of the Soviet leadership under the pressures of a malfunctioning domestic system and of foreign resistance by the industrialized democracies and by Third World nationalism. A second factor is the fiscal constraints in the United States and in the Soviet Union. Another is the increased relative economic weight of U.S. allies and their own reaction to perceived changes in the U.S.S.R. Whatever course the new Administration may take, its policymakers would be well advised to consider the factors analyzed and the conclusions drawn in this book.

Harold Brown
Foreign Policy Institute
The Johns Hopkins University
September 1988

Acknowledgements

This volume is part of the Council on Foreign Relations Project on East-West Relations, which is supported by the Carnegie Corporation. This particular volume was made possible as well by a grant from the Schumann Foundation.

To assist the authors in writing the book the Council organized, in the first five months of 1988, four seminars on different aspects of the arms control process, which were chaired by Harold Brown.

A series of background papers was prepared for the meetings. The subjects and authors were as follows:

"The Reagan Legacy," R. Jeffrey Smith, *The Washington Post*
"The Gorbachev Approach," Coit D. Blacker, University of Southern California
"Strategic Offensive Forces," David Ochmanek, The Rand Corporation
"Strategic Defense," Arnold Kanter, The Rand Corporation
"Conventional Arms Control," Joshua Epstein, The Brookings Institution

The authors and the Council are grateful to those who wrote these papers, to those who took part in the seminars, to Harold Brown and Jan M. Lodal, who read the entire manuscript and provided helpful comments and suggestions, and to Cynthia Paddock for organizing it. Michael Mandelbaum deserves special mention because he conceived the project, provided constant guidance to the study group, and contributed generously with both substantive and editorial advice to the authors.

William H. Gleysteen
Vice President, Studies
Council on Foreign Relations

1

Introduction and Setting— Cooperation and Competition

RELATIONS BETWEEN THE United States and the Soviet Union, its chief adversary, are, at the close of the Reagan administration, changing rapidly. Activities that would have been nearly inconceivable just four years ago are being undertaken in 1988 virtually without controversy. As this book goes to press, teams from both nations are observing the destruction of Pershing II and SS-20 missiles, American scientists and officials are installing monitoring devices at the Soviets' nuclear weapons test site near Semipalatinsk in Central Asia, and Soviet troops are withdrawing from Afghanistan, leaving the regime in Kabul on its own to face the Mujahadeen.

Arms control agreements—negotiated limitations on the size, character, activities, and deployments of military forces—over the past three decades, have played a growing role both in U.S.–Soviet relations and in East–West relations generally. By all indications, this growth will continue. As President Reagan and his advisers learned, the arms control process has, for better or worse, taken on a life of its own: No administration can afford to eschew or ignore arms control as an element of its diplomatic strategy. Even in 1983–1984, when U.S.–Soviet antagonisms had reached their highest levels in recent years, the administration deemed it advisable to adopt a forthcoming attitude toward East–West arms control, in effect inviting Moscow back to the negotiating table whenever it wished to come.

Yet, while the arms control process seems to have matured into a hardy perennial (some might call it a noxious weed), arms control as an effective instrument in shaping the East–West military balance remains something of a hothouse plant, its vitality subject to the vagaries of the broader political climate. Washington's refusal to ratify the SALT II treaty, for example, had less to do with any limitations or defects in the treaty itself than with exogenous factors, including the Soviet

1

invasion of Afghanistan and widespread acceptance among Americans of the view that the United States had allowed the Soviet Union to achieve a potentially dangerous level of military superiority. Likewise, agreement on a treaty to eliminate longer-range intermediate nuclear forces (INF) missiles, though manifestly in Moscow's interest, had to await the coming to power of a flexible, perceptive Soviet leader determined to reverse traditional patterns of Soviet political-military strategy.

In this book, we explore what are likely to be the most important issues on the arms control agenda for the next administration and beyond. We examine the broad basis for the continuing U.S.–Soviet dialogue on arms control, as well as the concrete forms that U.S.–Soviet arms control talks are likely to take, focusing in particular on the key choices that will face the next president and his advisers.

In the course of this review, we examine the prospects for and the implications of agreements that would limit strategic nuclear forces (both offensive and defensive), forces deployed in Europe, antisatellite and chemical weapons, and nuclear testing. We consider both *structural* and *operational* arms control measures. Structural arms control measures, including the U.S.–Soviet Intermediate Nuclear Forces Treaty of 1987, the Antiballistic Missile (ABM) Treaty of 1972, and the agreements limiting strategic offensive arms that emerged from the Strategic Arms Limitation Talks in 1972 and 1979, are designed to limit, shape, and in some cases reduce the military arsenals of the signatories. Operational arms control agreements, by contrast, place limits on the activities and deployments of military forces. For example, the agreement on confidence- and security-building measures (CSBMs) signed in Stockholm in 1987 commits its signatories, among other things, to provide advance notification of certain military training exercises. Such measures are intended to constrain the combat potential of forces in their day-to-day deployment postures, and to provide greater transparency and predictability regarding the location, readiness status, and training activities of these forces, thus reducing opportunities for successful surprise attack.

U.S. and Soviet National Security Objectives

The prominent role played by arms control in the security policies of Western and Eastern governments is in large measure a result of the fundamental reality of security in the nuclear age: Both superpowers have the capacity to *destroy* but not to *disarm* each other by force of arms. Thus, neither side can feel secure unless the other does as well.

Yet, at the same time each superpower retains geopolitical interests that are, at least to some degree, at odds with the other's. The tension between these two conditions has made it difficult for the West to sustain a policy toward Moscow and its allies that adequately addresses the two sides of the East–West relationship: the need for cooperation and the existence of competition.

Common Ground

Members of the two opposing alliance systems, the North Atlantic Treaty Organization (NATO) and the Warsaw Pact, have (or *should* have) clear-cut interests in common regarding the ongoing arms competition and the maintenance of peace and independence. In our view, these common interests can be expressed as the desire to strengthen three types of stability: crisis, or first-strike, stability; arms race stability; and political stability.

At the most basic level, the opposing superpowers and their alliance partners wish to avoid a nuclear war, the consequences of which would be truly catastrophic. Thus, both sides are deeply interested in strengthening what has been called crisis stability or first-strike stability. That is, they would like to reduce the likelihood of any direct military conflict between the superpowers by strengthening the long-standing retaliatory deterrent stalemate. Deterrence rests on the clear recognition by both sides that the enormous costs and risks associated with the use of nuclear weapons would outweigh any possible gains. The stability of this condition can be strengthened by reducing both the pressures and the incentives that the decision-makers on each side might feel to launch a major offensive against the other or to get in the first nuclear blow.

Structural arms control measures can contribute to first-strike stability by reducing the attack potential of both sides, while simultaneously permitting them to maintain forces for effective conventional defense and for punishing nuclear retaliation. Operational arms control can increase stability by establishing procedures and mechanisms to increase the timeliness and clarity of information available to decision-makers on both sides, thus reducing the likelihood that war will occur "by mistake."

East and West have a common interest in achieving arms race stability as well. Increasingly, the two sides have come to recognize that further expansions of their military arsenals do not necessarily produce greater security. Thus, they have sought increasingly to slow, channel, halt, or avoid particular aspects of the arms competition. This perspective is most evident in the policies of the United States and the Soviet

Union toward the massive strategic nuclear arsenals they both deploy. The leaders of both superpowers seem at last to have concluded that their adversary will do whatever is necessary to prevent the attainment by the other of clear-cut strategic nuclear superiority.* Thus, they apparently have come to value the reciprocal restraint and greater predictability that strategic arms control agreements can bring to the evolution of central strategic nuclear arsenals.

Nuclear states whose strategic arsenals are one-fiftieth to one-twentieth the size of those of the superpowers—the United Kingdom, France, and China—are not yet prepared to agree to freeze or reduce the size of their nuclear forces. However, they have all indicated a willingness to consider such reductions once the superpowers have made very major reductions in their own strategic nuclear forces.

A quite different situation has obtained in the realm of conventional forces. In particular, it seems far less certain that the nations of the Warsaw Pact or, for that matter, NATO are prepared to cap and reduce their large conventional forces in pursuit of arms race stability. The Soviet Union has long relied on its massive ground and air forces as the cornerstone of its power and influence vis-a-vis its European and Asian neighbors. And NATO is understandably chary of reducing its forces in the shadow of Warsaw Pact numerical superiority. Yet, as General Secretary Gorbachev's influence has strengthened and spread, the West has heard repeated Soviet declarations about the bankruptcy of previous Soviet overreliance upon military power and about the need to conclude agreements that produce drastic reductions in and a radical restructuring of the theater conventional forces of both the Warsaw Pact and NATO. Thus, the pursuit of arms race stability may be taking on additional momentum in the conventional arms arena as well.

Finally, the members of the opposing alliance systems have a shared interest in increased political stability in their relations with one another. The Soviet Union, led by Mr. Gorbachev, seeks a more benign

---

* Superiority in the realm of strategic nuclear forces could manifest itself in two ways: a massive degree of numerical superiority in terms of deployed weapons and launchers, or a one-sided capacity to draw down an adversary's nuclear forces such that his retaliatory attack could, at worst, inflict damage that might be deemed "acceptable." The latter could be achieved through the deployment of highly effective offensive weapons, defensive weapons, or both in combination. The United States enjoyed a condition of strategic nuclear superiority in the 1950s and early 1960s, at least in the first, numerical sense.

and predictable international environment in order to facilitate the chances for success in the daunting task of revitalizing its economic and political system. Gorbachev may also calculate that the Soviet Union can most effectively protect and advance its long-term security interests through a flexible, activist foreign policy in an atmosphere of renewed East–West détente. In the United States and other Western countries, there is similar enthusiasm for improved East–West relations. And while some in the West fear that complacency, not to say euphoria, in the wake of a return to détente may undermine the West's willingness to sustain an adequate defense posture, we detect a more general assumption that, given deep-seated Soviet and East European economic and political difficulties, the West is likely to gain from a period of competitive but nonconfrontational coexistence.

The successful conclusion of major arms control agreements, such as the SALT agreements and the ABM treaty, and sustained compliance with them, generally has had a positive "spillover" effect on the broader East–West political relationship. Advances in the bilateral arms control process can encourage cooperation in other areas, including crisis avoidance and crisis management, expanded economic and cultural relations, and, importantly, mutual restraint in regional conflicts.

The political leaderships on both sides also seek a more stable and cooperative bilateral relationship because they would like to contain and, if possible, reduce defense spending. In Washington, this desire has been intensified by the need to control the very large federal deficit. In Moscow, Gorbachev badly needs additional investment resources to support his efforts to modernize capital stocks—a critical aspect of his economic *perestroika* (restructuring) strategy—even as he attempts to raise living standards.

In one sense, economic payoffs from bilateral reductions in theater and strategic nuclear forces are likely to be relatively modest. As we shall see, the United States will almost certainly find it necessary to implement several central strategic force modernization programs, even under a regime of START reductions. And the comprehensive verification measures associated with the INF and Strategic Arms Reduction Talks (START) agreements will be expensive. On the other hand, the ABM treaty, which allows ballistic missile research and development activities but bans the deployment of large ABM systems for nationwide defense, has arguably saved both sides tens of billions of dollars that might otherwise have been spent in competitive deployments of ballistic missile defenses (BMD) and offensive countermeasures. Maintenance of the ABM treaty regime would represent an extremely important cost avoidance measure for both the Soviet Union and the United States.

Major cuts in the Soviet Union's massive theater conventional forces, be they a result of forthcoming NATO–Warsaw Pact talks or of Soviet unilateral actions, could produce a substantial reduction in Soviet defense expenditures. These savings would come from reduced operating and maintenance costs of the units cut and from avoidance of the costs of reequipping these units with newer weapon systems.

Unilateral Soviet Interests

Not all U.S. and Soviet objectives in arms control run in parallel, cooperative directions. The United States and the Soviet Union also pursue competitive interests as they seek to gain advantages at each other's expense.

Mr. Gorbachev insists that the "new political thinking" that has emerged in Moscow over the past few years has led the Soviet Union to reconsider its outlook on world affairs, and to alter its objectives accordingly. Despite these claims, Gorbachev continues to pursue vigorously what have long been the primary international security objectives of Soviet leaders. These include the desires to accomplish the following:

- Reduce drastically the role of nuclear weapons in the East–West military competition. This would serve to weaken the credibility of the U.S. "flexible response" doctrine in Europe and elsewhere, thus undermining the American extended nuclear deterrent and enhancing the peacetime coercive value and potential wartime utility of the Soviet Union's massive conventional forces.
- Promote the withdrawal of U.S. theater nuclear and conventional forces from Europe and other areas, including the Persian Gulf and the Asian–Pacific region. Such withdrawals would make these areas much more vulnerable to Soviet intimidation.
- Break up Western unity, focusing on U.S. relations with its NATO allies in Western Europe.
- Win the battle for world public opinion by portraying the Soviet Union as the more "reasonable" superpower, sincerely committed to easing international tensions and halting the arms race.

While Gorbachev's overall approach to foreign, arms control, and defense policy has been much more subtle and flexible than that of his predecessors, all of these objectives are well served by Gorbachev's initiatives.

The Soviets have also consistently put forward arms control proposals crafted to further their own immediate defense objectives. Although in most cases they have failed to achieve these aims, they have persisted in seeking to do the following:

- Constrain or ban those U.S. systems that pose the greatest military challenge to the Soviet Union. The Soviets have, at one time or another, sought to ban the deployment of air-, sea-, and ground-launched cruise missiles; the Pershing II intermediate-range ballistic missile; the MX intercontinental ballistic missile (ICBM); the D-5 submarine-launched ballistic missile (SLBM), and the B-2 "stealth" bomber. In recent years they have concentrated their efforts on severely constraining the development and banning the deployment of the multitiered ballistic missile defense system being pursued under the Reagan administration's Strategic Defense Initiative (SDI).
- Avoid or minimize constraints on the military programs of greatest value to the Soviet Union, such as the SS-18 class heavy ICBMs and the new mobile SS-24 and SS-25 ICBMs.
- Gain compensation in U.S.–Soviet arms control agreements for U.S. forward-based fighter-bombers deployed at overseas bases or on aircraft carriers and for the nuclear delivery systems of the United Kingdom, France, and China. All of these weapons could strike Soviet territory, and no comparable threat is directed at the United States. Thus, Moscow has sought to count these weapons against U.S. quotas during negotiations on the SALT, INF, and START treaties.

Unilateral American Interests

The pursuit of arms control agreements is but one dimension of U.S. national security policy. In tandem with arms control initiatives, the United States, like the Soviet Union, seeks to advance its fundamental security interests through a combination of unilateral and cooperative efforts to maintain and increase Western military strength. The United States, for example, would like to conclude arms agreements that would significantly reduce the current Soviet military superiority in theaters around the Soviet periphery and thus reduce the Kremlin's potential for intimidation in Western Europe and elsewhere. Significant force reductions in Eastern Europe and the change in political climate that would likely accompany them might also serve to loosen Moscow's grip on Eastern Europe.

At the same time, the United States, in concert with its major allies, must maintain adequate nuclear and conventional forces to underwrite its strategy of flexible response. This strategy seeks to deter aggression by confronting an attacker with opposition by sizable conventional forces as well as with threats to use nuclear weapons, if necessary, at a level appropriate to the enemy's military provocation.

The accomplishments of the East–West arms control process to date have been quite modest. Even assuming the superpowers succeed in concluding a START treaty along the lines that have largely been agreed upon, each side will retain thousands of strategic nuclear weapons. And despite some promising new developments, the prospects for really substantial reductions in the levels of military forces deployed in Europe during the next several years are not great. Even if implemented, bilateral reductions in Europe would almost certainly leave NATO and the Warsaw Pact with considerable capabilities for large-scale military operations against each other.

Consequently, even in the best of circumstances, it will be necessary for the United States and its allies to proceed with a number of ongoing nuclear and conventional force modernization programs. For example, the United States will continue to require a survivable and effective strategic nuclear retaliatory capability. This will necessitate continued attention to strategic force modernization, with or without arms control. Options available to the next administration include fielding some form of mobile ICBM, deploying additional Trident submarines carrying long-range C-4 or D-5 SLBMs, and adding the B-2 bomber with its unique stealth capabilities to evade Soviet air defenses.

Likewise, even given rapid progress toward reductions in Warsaw Pact forces, some measures designed to strengthen NATO's conventional defense capabilities will be called for. Major options here include the deployment of sophisticated surveillance sensors, such as the airborne Joint Surveillance and Target Attack Radar System (JSTARS) to track enemy ground force movements; computerized systems for correlation and display of surveillance data; new, long-range delivery systems, such as the F-15E fighter-bomber and Army Tactical Missile System (ATACMS); and a variety of specialized weapons and munitions that can disable tanks, crater and mine runways, and destroy bunkers and bridges.

In short, as the United States and its allies pursue arms control negotiations with the Soviet Union and the Warsaw Pact, the Western countries will seek to preserve options to improve unilaterally the capabilities of their military forces.

The Contemporary Arms Control Environment

The Reagan Legacy

After nearly eight years, the Reagan administration has left a substantial imprint on American arms control policy. Somewhat ironically, arms control at the close of the Reagan era is seen as a central and legitimate element of U.S. national security policy across the American political spectrum. Ronald Reagan came to office as, at best, an avowed skeptic and often a vigorous opponent of most previous U.S.–Soviet arms control agreements and negotiations. Arms control, he and his supporters claimed, had not made the United States more secure. Rather, they declared, arms control agreements had failed to reduce Soviet military strength while at the same time lulling the West into a false sense of security and a reduced willingness to support costly defense programs.

Yet President Reagan concluded a landmark nuclear arms limitation agreement, the INF treaty, that, for better or worse, will produce an unprecedented reduction in the nuclear arsenals of the superpowers. The treaty will completely eliminate an entire class of U.S. and Soviet nuclear delivery systems—land-based ballistic and cruise missiles with ranges of 300–3000 miles—and provides by far the most comprehensive and intrusive verification measures yet agreed to by the superpowers for monitoring treaty compliance.

Moreover, Mr. Reagan has become a strong advocate of further, even more significant U.S.–Soviet arms reduction agreements. The Reagan administration will almost certainly bequeath to its successor a nearly completed START treaty that goes far beyond what many thought possible eight years ago. It may also leave behind an agreed mandate for the conduct of a new set of negotiations between the members of NATO and the Warsaw Pact on the reduction of conventional forces throughout Europe. (Progress to date on START and on the framework for the new European conventional stability talks are discussed in chapters 2 and 4.)

Perhaps unwittingly, President Reagan has helped to bring about a significant reversal in public perceptions about how best to deal with the Soviet military threat. Compared with the situation in the early 1980s, it will be easier for President Reagan's successors—Democrat or Republican—to work to contain that threat through arms reduction negotiations, and more difficult for them to redress imbalances by means of a large-scale military buildup. This reversal reflects not only Mr. Reagan's own changed attitude and accomplishments in the arms control arena but also a widespread sense that the massive defense buildup of the early 1980s has run its course. The substantial increase in the national debt and the prospect of continuing large federal deficits left behind by the Reagan administration have placed added pressure on U.S. defense programs and provide greater incentives for cuts in forces.

President Reagan will pass on to his successor a comparatively favorable political relationship between the United States and the Soviet Union—a rare accomplishment in the postwar world. This atmosphere will facilitate the pursuit of cooperative efforts to increase the security of both powers, chief among these being arms control agreements.

With regard to the conduct of arms control negotiations, the Reagan administration followed an "arm to parley" strategy throughout its first term. It placed top priority on implementing an extensive American arms buildup as a precondition to the successful negotiation of major arms reduction agreements with the Soviet Union. Whatever one's judgment about the efficacy of this approach, the pressures on the U.S. defense budget from the huge federal deficit that is, at least in part, a result of the Reagan defense buildup, largely rule out a similar strategy for Mr. Reagan's successor.

The hallmark of the Reagan administration's negotiating approach has been to demand deep reductions in those aspects of Soviet/Warsaw Pact military capability that are of greatest concern to the West, such as Soviet ballistic missiles of various ranges and the Warsaw Pact's pronounced advantages over NATO in tanks and artillery. In several cases the Soviets and their allies have been called upon to make cuts that are considerably greater than those required of the West. American proposals for such deep and often asymmetric reductions have frequently been advanced and then adhered to without apparent concern for their near-term negotiability. In several cases, including the "double zero" outcome of the INF treaty and the Soviets' agreement to reduce drastically their ballistic missile warheads in START, the Soviets have ultimately proved willing to accept these proposals.

President Reagan's penchant for deep reductions in nuclear weapons is itself part of the legacy he will bequeath to his successors. The assertion that reductions per se are desirable has gone largely unchallenged in the American political debate, in part because strategic nuclear arsenals are so large. But future administrations will be well advised to examine this assumption critically before tabling further arms control proposals.

Additionally, the Reagan administration witnessed a broad expansion of the role of the Congress in the entire arms control process. The administration encouraged the special arms control oversight committees of the Congress to take an active role in monitoring the ongoing negotiations. Its senior policymakers spent enormous amounts of time (not always of their own volition) on Capitol Hill briefing members of Congress and their staffs on the latest developments in the various negotiations. Several members of the Congress took advantage of these and other opportunities to help shape U.S. negotiating and compliance policies.

In recent years the Congress has increasingly engaged in the practice of attaching amendments to the annual defense authorization and appropriations bills that limit the freedom of action of the executive branch in testing or deploying new weapons systems. These restrictions have been applied when majorities in the Congress judged a given activity as contrary to existing U.S. treaty obligations or unwise in light of potential negotiating opportunities.

The Senate displayed its newfound activism regarding arms control in its very detailed scrutiny of the INF treaty during the lengthy treaty ratification process. Most dramatically, the Senate successfully pressed the administration to reopen direct discussions with the Soviets aimed at clarifying certain portions of the treaty the Senate found ambiguous. Congressional involvement in the details of arms control was greatly intensified by the administration's reinterpretation of the ABM treaty—a reinterpretation the administration supported by stating that it was in no way bound by interpretations provided by the executive branch to the Senate during the original process of ratification.

The Reagan administration's handling of the ABM treaty's interpretation has been the source of its most negative influence on arms control. While congressionally imposed restrictions on the conduct of SDI flight-testing programs have limited the resulting damage to the treaty regime, President Reagan's persistent refusal to compromise on this issue may continue to inhibit progress toward a more stable strategic nuclear balance through arms control. By enunciating a "broad" interpretation of the ABM treaty, and by creating a political constituency for the deployment of large-scale ballistic missile defenses, President Reagan has ensured that his influence will be felt on these issues long after his departure from office.

More broadly, President Reagan's launching of the SDI has dramatically altered the debate about nuclear deterrence. It has sparked new interest in potential roles for ballistic missile defense and a wide-ranging reexamination of the whole concept of retaliatory deterrence as the basis for security, a subject we address in chapter 3.

The U.S.–Soviet dispute over SDI and the ABM treaty has, of course, already proven to be a major obstacle to the conclusion of a START agreement. And President Reagan's determined stand on this point may make it difficult for his successor to compromise on this controversial issue because of concerns about his ability to gain Senate ratification of any resulting START treaty.

Gorbachev's "New Thinking"

During the past three years Mikhail Gorbachev, the general secretary of the Soviet Communist Party, has stimulated an increasingly vigorous debate in Moscow about the future directions of Soviet foreign and security policy. He and several others have openly criticized previous Soviet policy perspectives and laid out a new set of ideas that they claim now guide Soviet international behavior and defense preparations. They refer to these ideas collectively as the new political thinking.

The central tenets of Secretary Gorbachev's new political thinking that have particular relevance to Soviet defense and arms control policy are these:

- Recognition of the growth of international interdependence. Cooperative action is said to be needed to deal with common ecological, economic, and security problems, including, above all, avoiding war, particularly nuclear war.
- Rejection of the pursuit of unilateral security by the Soviet Union. Where Soviet security was once viewed as enhanced only at the expense of the security of its adversaries, the new thinking asserts that security can only be mutual in the nuclear age.
- Admission that the Soviet Union has traditionally relied too heavily on military power in its dealings with other states and a call to place greater emphasis on diplomacy, negotiation, and other means to ensure Soviet security.
- Harsh condemnation of nuclear deterrence. While reliance on nuclear weapons is grudgingly acknowledged to be useful in the near term, it is said to be inherently unstable and exceptionally dangerous in the longer run.
- The declaration that Soviet military capabilities should be maintained at the level of "reasonable sufficiency" in support of a military doctrine for the Soviet Union and its Warsaw Pact allies that is said to be "strictly defensive."

Soviet discussions about the last element—reasonable sufficiency as the appropriate objective for Soviet defense preparations—have been under way since the fall of 1985. Top political leaders, civilian academic specialists, and senior military officers have been engaged in a lively debate about the meaning of "reasonable" or "defense" sufficiency as applied to both the strategic nuclear balance between the superpowers and the conventional balance between the forces of NATO and the Warsaw Pact.

This dialogue has obvious relevance for Soviet arms control policy. With regard to strategic nuclear forces, most Soviet military and civilian commentators have defined reasonable sufficiency in ways that support a policy of:

- Seeking deep cuts in the central strategic nuclear arsenals of the superpowers while maintaining rough numerical parity.
- Preserving the existing state of strategic stability between the superpowers. Soviet commentators have defined strategic stability as the prevailing situation in which the Soviet Union and the United States each have the capability to inflict "unacceptable damage" in retaliation against the other, even under worst-case circumstances (that is, after being subjected to a surprise, would-be disarming first strike).

Some Soviet civilian analysts have gone beyond this, suggesting that as long as the Soviet Union maintained "qualitative parity" with the United States—that is, a secure second-strike capability that could inflict unacceptable damage—there would be no need to be concerned about maintaining approximate numerical parity with the strategic nuclear forces of the United States.[1]

Unsurprisingly, senior Soviet military figures have consistently rejected the idea that the Soviet Union should settle for numerically inferior strategic forces, insisting instead that any reductions in strategic nuclear force levels must be mutual and roughly equal.[2] So long as this condition is met, however, the military has apparently been prepared since the early 1980s to support policies providing for deep and equitable cuts in nuclear forces.

Soviet spokesmen have also discussed the meaning of reasonable sufficiency—"sufficiency for defense," to use the Soviet military's preferred formulation—as applied to conventional forces, with particular reference to the NATO–Warsaw Pact balance in Europe. Initial formulations in this area simply equated sufficiency with the current Soviet/Warsaw Pact force posture, a posture described as adequate "to repulse aggression" and "to reliably ensure the collective defense of the socialist community."[3] Over time, however, the emphasis in discussions of reasonable sufficiency in the theater has shifted from a present to a future orientation. Increasingly, in fact, the concept has come to be associated with an aspiration to reconfigure radically the military forces of both NATO and the Warsaw Pact in ways that would preclude a successful surprise attack by one on the other and ultimately would rule out the mounting of offensive operations altogether. The Soviets have sometimes described this objective as a cooperative transition on the part of the opposing alliances to a posture of "nonoffensive defense" or "defensive defense," borrowing a phrase from theorists associated with disarmament circles in Western Europe.

When pressed for details regarding what a reasonably sufficient posture in Central Europe might look like, Soviet civilian analysts have readily admitted that they are in the very earliest stages of exploring this concept. Soviet analysts who advocate the idea of reasonable sufficiency are seeking to develop a concept of stability for conventional force balances analogous to the unacceptable damage threshold they are using to define strategic stability in the U.S.–Soviet nuclear balance.

Soviet discussions of new political thinking and reasonable or defense sufficiency have been accompanied by an activist, détente-oriented foreign policy and a wide-ranging and ambitious set of arms control initiatives. Mr. Gorbachev has established himself personally in the West as a vigorous, innovative, and apparently flexible figure, eager to reduce East–West military confrontation and to conclude a host of far-reaching arms control agreements.

The Soviet leader's bold, new arms control agenda has both utopian and pragmatic features. On the utopian side, it calls for the worldwide abolition of nuclear weapons by the year 2000, a comprehensive ban on nuclear testing, and the radical restructuring of NATO and Warsaw Pact theater forces so that neither side could launch an effective surprise attack or even conduct large-scale offensive operations. While pushing this visionary approach, with its obvious public diplomacy benefits, the Soviets have also made more practical proposals, which are described in the chapters that follow.

Perhaps the most dramatic change in the Soviets' pragmatic behavior has been the startling shift in their approach to verification. Where not so long ago the Soviet Union, for reasons of military secrecy, strongly resisted intrusive, on-site inspections, today its spokesmen boldly claim that they are prepared for any and all verification measures, including short-notice, on-site inspections at any time and any place.[4] They have matched this rhetoric with concrete proposals for extensive and intrusive verification measures in various negotiations and have agreed to unprecedented verification provisions in the INF treaty and the Stockholm agreement on confidence- and security-building measures. These include the establishment of a permanent U.S. monitoring presence outside a major Soviet missile production facility; short-notice challenge inspections of missile storage, testing, and deployment areas; and on-site inspections of major military exercises on Soviet territory.

There are widely differing views in the West regarding the real significance of Soviet new political thinking and the debates in Moscow about reasonable sufficiency. Without question, Mr. Gorbachev and his colleagues have set a bold new course for Soviet defense and arms control policy. The Soviet leadership has come to realize, probably following a fundamental reassessment, that the approach of the past, in which the Soviet Union appeared determined to amass sufficient military power to surpass and overawe its adversaries, is no longer useful. The new leadership has chosen instead to adopt a more subtle, flexible approach that seeks to diminish Western perceptions of the military threat posed by the Soviet Union and thus weaken Western collective defense exertions. Soviet arms control diplomacy plays a major role in this effort.

Moreover, Stephen M. Meyer, an American academic specialist in Soviet foreign and defense policy, suggests that Gorbachev's reasonable sufficiency campaign has a significant domestic policy component as well.[5] According to this interpretation, in the midst of his enormously difficult tasks of seeking to revive the stagnant Soviet economy and to revitalize Soviet society, Mr. Gorbachev is determined to reassert Party primacy in the defense arena. Under Leonid Brezhnev, the processes of establishing basic security objectives, assessing external threats, elaborating doctrinal concepts, defining military requirements, developing force programs and assessing their relative effectiveness, all rested almost exclusively in the hands of the Ministry of Defense. By raising questions about basic, national security assumptions and sponsoring a far-reaching debate about crucial aspects of Soviet defense policy—a debate whose participants include for the first time a group of civilian academics as well as the usual military professionals—Secretary Gorbachev is moving to recapture control of the national security agenda. If he is successful, the prospects for lasting changes in Moscow's security objectives will be significantly enhanced.

All of the Soviet talk about new thinking on foreign and security policy and reasonable sufficiency for defense may be, as some fear, nothing more than a cunning tactic that makes use of jargon and concepts borrowed from the West to support a strategy designed to serve traditional Soviet expansionist objectives. Alternatively, it may reflect, as we suspect, a willingness to contemplate seriously a fundamental redefinition of Soviet security objectives in the international political environment. If the latter is the case, Mr. Gorbachev's ascendancy presents significant opportunities to conclude far-reaching bilateral and multilateral agreements to reduce, redeploy, and disengage the military forces on both sides in ways that allow East and West to maintain or increase their security with lower levels of forces.

At the same time, there remains a danger that the Soviets—now much more dynamic and flexible than previously—will use arms control negotiations and the public diplomacy surrounding them to undermine the cohesiveness of the Western alliance and to decrease Western military power relative to that of the Soviet Union and the Warsaw Pact.

The challenge to U.S. and allied policymakers is to put forward arms control proposals that seriously test Mr. Gorbachev's willingness to translate his bold words into concrete deeds. The West must do so with offers that would strengthen first-strike stability, contain and channel the arms competition in safer directions, and promote a more cooperative relationship between East and West. At the same time, the West must avoid crafting proposals whose primary purpose is to score public relations points, and it must beware of unwarranted euphoria about the ability of arms control agreements to act as a substitute for maintenance of an adequate defense capability. For while such agreements may reduce the military capabilities of the Soviet Union, they cannot eliminate them.

2

START—Still the Centerpiece

CONTROLLING THE SIZE of their intercontinental-range nuclear forces—ICBMs, SLBMs, and heavy bombers—remains the central focus of the superpowers' arms control dialogue. Before assessing the prospects for completion of a START agreement and evaluating the treaty's impact on strategic nuclear forces and U.S. security, it is useful to review the reasons that the United States and the Soviet Union have entered into negotiations to limit these forces.

The Purposes of START

Independent of whatever unilateral national interests might be served by arms control (a subject we shall turn to in a moment), negotiated limitations on the long-range strategic nuclear arsenals of the superpowers are intended, above all, to reduce the risks of war—especially nuclear war—by strengthening stability in three dimensions: arms race stability, political stability, and first-strike, or crisis, stability.

Arms Race Stability

Arms control agreements constrain and channel the U.S.–Soviet arms competition in predictable directions by capping and, as they have recently, reducing overall force size and banning some weapons deployments. In an era when each of the superpowers deploys many thousands of nuclear warheads, leaders on both sides have come to the conclusion that deploying still more warheads will not lead to a commensurate increase in security, particularly if one's opponent is determined to deploy a roughly equal number, as has been the case. Bilat-

17

eral agreements to halt and then reverse the growth of nuclear arsenals, then, provide an opportunity for both participants to maintain
their security at equal, lower levels of forces.

The limits on strategic nuclear delivery vehicles contained in SALT I
and SALT II have helped to constrain the competitive expansion of the
U.S. and Soviet ICBM, SLBM, and bomber forces. Yet, the number of
strategic warheads (or weapons) deployed by both sides has expanded
dramatically since the early 1970s, primarily because of the widespread
introduction of multiple, independently targeted reentry vehicles
(MIRVs) on ICBMs and SLBMs. By restricting the number of launchers
deployed but not their size or the number of weapons they carry, the
SALT accords encouraged this development. The emerging START
agreement would cap the number of deployed weapons and, indeed,
reverse this growth.

Political Stability

By concluding and complying with strategic arms limitation agreements, the United States and the Soviet Union demonstrate that they
can take advantage of their shared interests in limiting the arms competition and avoiding war. The political spillover of the ABM and SALT
treaties has had, on balance, clear benefits in the broader East–West
relationship. In particular, the arms control process has helped to
sustain an atmosphere between Moscow and Washington that facili-
tates cooperation rather than conflict in a host of areas, including crisis
avoidance and crisis management, mutual restraint in regional conflicts, economic and cultural relations, and other bilateral matters.

Of course, some observers criticize the arms control process for just
this reason. They view arms control as a soporific that lulls the West
into a sense of complacency about the nature of the Soviet threat,
making it more difficult to sustain support for defense programs even if
they are permitted by the arms control regime. Seen from this perspective, the political spillover resulting from the arms control process is a
reason *not* to play the arms control game.

First-Strike (Crisis) Stability

Finally, START is intended to help strengthen the prevailing retaliatory
deterrent stalemate, under which both the United States and the Soviet
Union are dissuaded from using nuclear weapons because the costs
and risks associated with such use would clearly outweigh any potential gains. Through unilateral force deployments, the superpowers
have succeeded in fielding secure second-strike forces that can survive
and inflict catastrophic damage on an enemy even following a surprise

first strike. Both superpowers will no doubt remain determined to retain these capabilities.

Strategic arms control can help make this stalemate more stable in the face of technological changes, misperceptions, and other uncertainties by reducing the attack potential of both sides. A combination of reductions in force size and restrictions on the development of certain capabilities can make it easier for both sides to deploy their forces in survivable ways. Reductions and selective restrictions alone, however, do not ensure improved first-strike stability. As we shall see, deep bilateral cuts in forces could, in fact, result in significantly reduced retaliatory capabilities if the resulting forces are not based in survivable ways.

Thus, reductions must be implemented such that the forces remaining under the treaty regime are adequate in numbers and capabilities to credibly hold at risk those things the adversary values most highly—its military forces, urban-industrial infrastructure, and institutions of political and administrative control—even following a surprise first strike. In addition to imposing reductions, then, arms control agreements must permit their signatories to improve the survivability of their retaliatory strike systems.

Additionally, many students of first-strike stability have concluded that maintaining a credible threat of unacceptable retaliation alone (what might be termed stability I) is insufficient to assure first-strike stability under all conditions. States do not always begin wars in order to achieve objectives whose value is judged at the outset to exceed by a sufficient margin the estimated costs associated with prosecuting the war. Indeed, states may attack one another because their leaders believe they have no alternatives that are more attractive (or, more to the point, less unattractive) than going to war.*

Regarding strategic nuclear forces, such a desperate perspective could pertain in a deep crisis if the forces deployed by one or both sides were sufficiently vulnerable that *the costs associated with executing a first strike were perceived as greatly exceeded by the costs of refraining from the*

---

* By way of example, Thucydides tells us that the Spartans declared war on Athens despite serious misgivings about their ability to prevail over the more wealthy and powerful Athenians. They took this desperate step, he writes, "because they were afraid of the further growth of Athenian power, seeing . . . that the greater part of Hellas was under the control of Athens." Thucydides, *History of the Peloponnesian War*, New York, Penguin Books, 1972, pp. 82–87. In a more modern context, the Japanese decision to risk all and declare war on the United States must have been influenced to some degree by a perception that no other available alternatives were less unattractive.

first strike (and thereby, perhaps, absorbing one's opponent's first strike). Again, a first strike might be launched in such a case even though the attacker was nearly certain that he would suffer in retaliation damage that was, to some extent, "unacceptable." (An attack of, say, 100 weapons, terrible though it would be, might well be regarded as far less unacceptable than an attack of 10,000 weapons.) This focus on the *relative* difference among war outcomes versus the *absolute* results of a nuclear exchange might be called stability II. The practical implication of this reasoning is that in order to assure maximal first strike stability both sides must deploy their forces in ways that prevent their opponent not only from being able to prevent a sizable retaliation (stability I), but also from being able to shift radically the balance of forces in his favor via a counterforce first strike (stability II).

Other Common Objectives

Arms control agreements have traditionally been intended to achieve other objectives as well. These have included *reducing the economic costs* of deploying adequate military forces and *reducing the consequences of war*, that is, the damage resulting should deterrence fail and war occur. Given the need to maintain a survivable, effective triad of strategic nuclear forces (that is, ICBMs, SLBMs, and bombers or cruise missiles), near-term cost savings resulting from a START agreement are likely to be modest. START, for example, will not materially reduce the importance of continuing to modernize the U.S. fleet of ballistic missile submarines. Nor will it entirely solve the problem of ICBM silo vulnerability. Thus, costly programs to address these needs will continue with or without START.

In addition, implementing the extensive measures needed to monitor Soviet compliance with treaty limits will be an expensive proposition. These measures will include deploying new reconnaissance satellites and installing sophisticated monitoring and communications equipment at key facilities inside the Soviet Union. Nevertheless, the price of maintaining adequate U.S. strategic nuclear forces under a START agreement would certainly be lower over the long term than that required to provide similarly effective forces in an environment characterized by an unconstrained U.S.–Soviet arms race.

Arms control agreements will not, in the foreseeable future, reduce the destructive capacity of the American and Soviet nuclear arsenals sufficiently to meaningfully affect either side's ability to inflict catastrophic damage on the other's assets. Indeed, first-strike stability, as defined above, demands that the arsenals *not* be so reduced. Certainly the United States is not at this time prepared to move away from today's "offense-dominant" world, in which assured retaliation provides the basis for deterrence of nuclear and large-scale conventional war. Thus, a START agreement should not be judged by the degree to which it would mitigate the effects of a major nuclear exchange.*

Finally, the serious pursuit of limitations on strategic nuclear forces—perhaps the single most important factor conferring superpower status—serves important symbolic objectives for both the United States and the Soviet Union. The negotiations are viewed—and widely applauded—by international as well as domestic audiences as evidence that the two giants are committed to reducing the risks of war and muting their geopolitical conflicts in the broader interests of peace. In the United States this has proven helpful to a series of administrations in countering antipathy toward the strategy of retaliatory deterrence in general and resistance to particular strategic nuclear force modernization programs. Rightly or wrongly, START helps to foster the impression that the leaders of both superpowers have the arms race under control and that progress is being made in the pursuit of a safer world.

Opposing Objectives

We assume that the purposes of START addressed above are shared, to greater or lesser degrees, by the United States and the Soviet Union. Naturally, the two nations also bring opposing interests and objectives to START and other arms control negotiations. Some of these were mentioned in chapter 1.

Particularly worthy of note here is the impact of the U.S. strategy of flexible response on its preferences toward strategic nuclear forces and arms control. The United States today pursues first-strike stability in the presence of other, competing objectives. In particular, it seeks to maintain the credibility of (largely implicit) threats to use nuclear weapons first, if necessary, to prevent a successful invasion of allied nations in Europe and elsewhere. The United States calls on its strate-

---

* Pending a transition to a defense-dominant world (see chapter 3), the prospects for meaningful damage limitation in the event of war would turn primarily on intrawar nuclear escalation control—that is, restraint on the part of both superpowers in conducting nuclear strikes, once a war had begun. These prospects could be enhanced through bilateral discussions in peacetime that sensitize both sides to the difficulties associated with exercising restraint while carrying out unilateral nuclear strike plans in a terribly unfavorable environment. Cooperative measures to maintain reliable communications between the sides during a nuclear war could also help to limit and rapidly terminate the conflict.

gic nuclear forces not only to deter attacks on its territory but also, in conjunction with nuclear and conventional forces deployed abroad, to "extend" deterrence to the protection of allies. U.S. nuclear forces help to offset the effects of sizable Soviet advantages in conventional forces in areas around the periphery of the Soviet Union. This requirement for credible (or, more properly, not wholly incredible) first-use options means that the United States will resist arms control proposals (such as very deep reductions to "minimal deterrent" forces) that might leave it without militarily useful nuclear employment options.

Beyond this rather basic difference, both nations bring other divergent objectives to the negotiations that lead them to try to further their own interests at the expense of each other. To a degree, this is the case in any negotiation: Each participant will try to get the best deal possible for himself.

In this case, the United States has sought to focus START reductions on Soviet ICBMs, especially heavy ICBMs of the SS-18 class. The Reagan administration has steadfastly maintained that ballistic missiles—particularly accurate ICBMs—should be singled out for reductions because they are inherently destabilizing. To the degree that these "fast fliers" are seen as the potential agents of a disarming first strike, they would, if launched, confront leaders with the need to make a decision in only a few minutes to "use or lose" their vulnerable forces.

The Reagan administration has also sought to reduce through START the Soviets' advantage in ICBM throwweight.* This advantage—around 3:1 today—provides the Soviets with the potential to deliver thousands more additional weapons against the United States than they have currently deployed, should they choose to replace their existing reentry vehicles (RVs) with new, lighter ones. The United States, on the other hand, deploys smaller missiles that already carry smaller and lighter RVs. It therefore does not have this option.

For their part, the Soviets seem to have brought a considerably broader list of their own interests to the START talks. Obviously, they have worked for an agreement that itself is favorable to their interests. For example, Soviet START proposals in the earliest days of General Secretary Gorbachev's tenure called for inclusion of American "forward-based systems" (fighter-bombers on aircraft carriers and on land in Europe and Asia) in strategic weapons totals. If accepted, this demand would have forced the United States either to reconfigure its theater- and carrier-based aviation forces or to deploy markedly fewer

---

* Throwweight is a measure of the lifting power of a ballistic missile. For a given range, the greater a missile's throwweight is, the heavier its payload can be.

strategic nuclear weapons than the Soviet Union does. Also, the Soviets continue to resist the imposition of a numerical sublimit on ICBM warheads—still the strong suit in their strategic nuclear forces.

Beyond these considerations, however, the Soviets appear to hope that START will further a gradual process of global denuclearization. We noted in chapter 1 our view that Moscow, recognizing the key role played by nuclear weapons in the U.S. strategy of flexible response, seems to have concluded that neutralizing the nuclear dimension of the East–West military balance would be in its interest. There is every reason to believe that Mr. Gorbachev has been sincere when he has proposed, at Reykjavik and elsewhere, that the United States and the Soviet Union eliminate all of their strategic nuclear weapons by the end of the century. This Soviet tendency to favor movement toward denuclearization—and the American determination to resist it—has led to several areas of disagreement in START, including counting rules for air-launched cruise missiles (ALCMs) and the treatment of sea-launched cruise missiles (SLCMs). In both cases, the Americans have shown a preference for more permissive limits, while the Soviets have pushed for constraints that would mandate smaller forces.

Finally, the Soviets are determined to retard efforts by the United States to develop and deploy space-based ballistic missile defenses. Unquestionably, the Soviets' insistence on linking START to a resolution of the meaning and duration of the ABM treaty has been the most serious obstacle to the completion of a START agreement.

Status of the Emerging START Treaty

As the Reagan administration draws to a close, many of the key elements of the START agreement are in place. In fact, the negotiators in Geneva have completed perhaps 90 percent of the detailed treaty drafting. The most critical limitations agreed to at present, along with their projected impact on the U.S.–Soviet central strategic nuclear balance, are as follows:

● *Fifty percent cuts/6000 "accountable weapons."*

The START treaty is being widely touted as an agreement that will cut the superpowers' existing strategic nuclear forces by 50 percent—that is, down from current levels of approximately 12,500 strategic weapons for the United States and some 11,000 for the Soviets to 6,000 weapons for each side. This is not the case. In fact, primarily because of a permissive provision for counting the weapons carried by penetrating bombers (those without ALCMs), each side would be likely to deploy a force of approximately 8,000–9,000 warheads on its ICBMs, SLBMs, and heavy bombers within the constraints of a START treaty—levels representing a 25–30 percent reduction from current levels.* Such strategic weapons totals under START would, however, be perhaps 40–50 percent lower than those projected by the mid-1990s in the absence of any arms control restraints. (See Figure 1.)

- *Subceiling of 4900 ICBM and SLBM RVs.*

This sublimit and the one-for-one counting procedure for weapons on existing missiles would produce a reduction of more than 50 percent in Soviet ballistic missile RVs. Specifically, under START, the Soviet Union would be compelled to cut to 4,900 the approximately 10,000 such weapons it currently fields. The reduction would be somewhat smaller for the United States: from approximately 8,000 RVs to 4,900.

- *Fifty percent cut in the Soviet heavy ICBMs of the SS-18 class and in Soviet ballistic missile throwweight.*

At long last, the Soviets have agreed to reduce by one-half their force of 308 silo-based missiles of the SS-18 class, which they were granted a unilateral right to deploy under SALT I in 1972. These behemoths possess approximately three times the throwweight of the next-largest ICBMs—the U.S. MX and the Soviet SS-19. Each SS-18 carries ten, and possibly as many as fourteen, RVs, and the SS-18 force comprises a substantial portion of Soviet ballistic missile throwweight (2.5 million kilograms out of a total of 5.6 million kilograms). Figure 2 shows the throwweight levels of current, START-constrained, and unconstrained U.S. and Soviet forces.

The elimination of half of the SS-18s, combined with the overall reduction in Soviet ICBMs and SLBMs to comply with the 4900 RV subceiling, would likely reduce overall Soviet missile throwweight

---

* The superpowers have agreed to a series of counting rules that will charge the RVs carried on ICBMs and SLBMs on a one-for-one basis. They have not yet agreed on how to count ALCMs carried by heavy bombers, as discussed in the section that follows on unresolved START issues, but the likely result will be at most a discount factor that counts one and one-half or two "actual" ALCMs as one accountable weapon. Each bomber not equipped with ALCMs would count as only *one* accountable weapon, even though large modern bombers can readily carry up to sixteen gravity bombs and short-range air-to-surface missiles. Thus, if either side were to deploy, say, 200 large non-ALCM bombers (B-1Bs, B-2s, Blackjacks), each carrying fourteen weapons, while remaining within the 6000 accountable weapons aggregate, it could field a force carrying 5800 ICBM and SLBM RVs and ALCMs plus 2800 bomber weapons (200 x 14), for a total force of 8600 actual weapons.

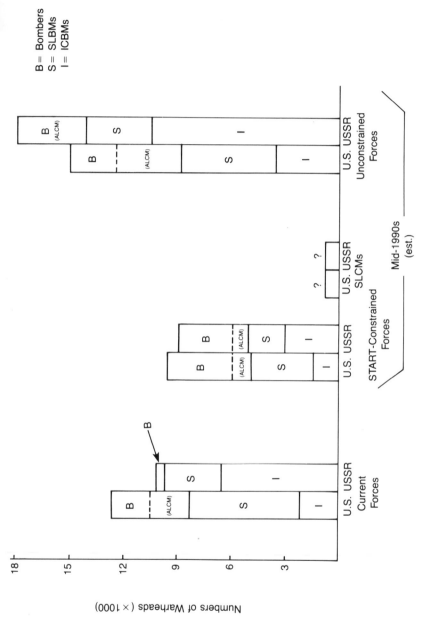

FIG. 1. *Comparative Levels of Strategic Nuclear Forces*

B = Bombers
S = SLBMs
I = ICBMs

Numbers of Warheads (× 1000)

18
15
12
9
6
3

U.S. USSR
Current
Forces

START-Constrained
Forces

U.S. USSR

U.S. USSR
SLCMs

Mid-1990s
(est.)

U.S. USSR
Unconstrained
Forces

25

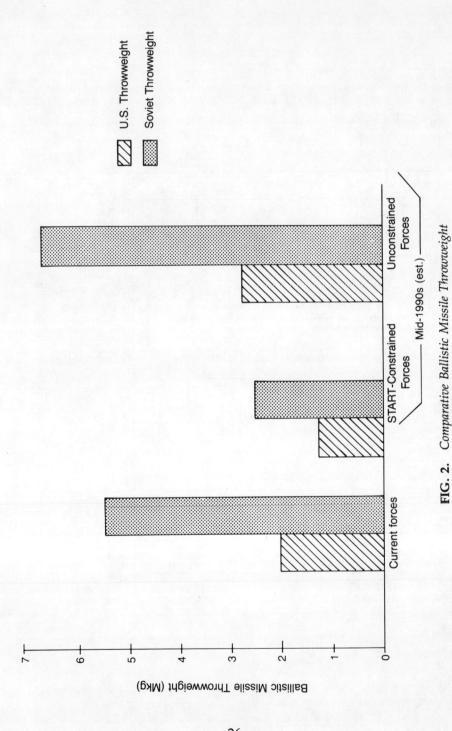

FIG. 2. *Comparative Ballistic Missile Throwweight*

26

from 5.6 to approximately 2.4 million kilograms. The Soviets have also agreed to a formal provision within the START treaty that would compel them to cut their ballistic missile throwweight by at least 50 percent. This reduction is desirable because it would limit the overall lifting power of the Soviet missile force that might be used to mount area barrage attacks against imprecisely located U.S. mobile ICBMs in the field or bombers as they seek to fly away from their bases.*

- *A ceiling of 1600 on strategic nuclear delivery vehicles (SNDVs).*

Both sides have agreed to reduce their delivery vehicles (that is, individual ballistic missiles and bombers) from current levels (approximately 2500 Soviet SNDVs and 2000 U.S. SNDVs) to 1600 or fewer.† To the degree that both sides continue to rely heavily on ICBMs and SLBMs that each carry several MIRVs, this launcher/platform limit would have little effect on force structure in light of the 4900 ballistic missile RV sublimit. However, should either side wish to deploy large numbers of smaller missiles, such as the Soviet SS-25 or the projected U.S. Midgetman ICBMs, each carrying one or two RVs, this limit might well constrain such deployments. Consequently, those who favor the deployment of smaller missiles as a means of enhancing ICBM survivability and strengthening first-strike stability rightly complain that the 1600 SNDV limit would hamper this de-MIRVing process.

Unresolved START Issues

Despite determined efforts by both sides through the summer of 1988 to resolve the issues that have blocked the signing of a START treaty, several thorny issues remain. We have already mentioned the problem of whether and how to link the START treaty to limits on the U.S. SDI and the fate of the ABM treaty, and will address it in detail in the next chapter. Other sticking points as of the time of this writing include the following:

---

* Barrage attacks would employ large numbers of nuclear explosions over a broad area in order to destroy whatever targets might be located there. This brute-force approach, though inefficient in terms of weapons destroyed versus weapons expended, would allow an attacker to destroy assets that it could not locate precisely, such as mobile ICBM launchers.

† The number of SNDVs attributed here to the United States does not include several hundred B-52 aircraft retired from active service and parked at the "boneyard" at Davis-Monthan Air Force Base in Arizona—aircraft that were counted under the provisions of the SALT treaties.

● *A separate limit on SLCMs.*

At Soviet insistence, the two sides agreed both at Reykjavik and again at the Washington summit to limit the number of long-range, nuclear-armed SLCMs. This limit would be independent of the ceiling on ICBM, SLBM, and bomber weapons. To date, however, Washington and Moscow have been unable to agree on the level of the SLCM ceiling. (The Soviets propose to limit deployments of SLCMs with a range greater than 600 kilometers to no more than 400 nuclear-armed SLCMs carried on two classes of submarines and one class of surface ship, and 600 conventionally armed SLCMs on agreed platforms. The United States has not tabled any proposals on SLCM force size.)

More important than the ceiling level, however, the United States insists that it cannot conceive of operationally acceptable yet reliable measures to verify any numerical limit on SLCMs, given U.S. plans to deploy not only some 750 long-range, nuclear-armed SLCMs but also more than 3000 long-range, conventionally armed SLCMs on approximately 200 surface ships and submarines.

● *Mobile ICBMs.*

The United States proposes to ban the deployment of mobile ICBMs by either side. Its position is based on considerations of verification difficulties, doubts about prospects for sustaining domestic political support for such deployments, and, somewhat perversely, a desire to deny the Soviet Union greater survivability for its ICBM force.* The Soviets have rejected this ban and are in the process of fielding the single-RV, road-mobile SS-25 and the ten-RV, rail-mobile SS-24. They have proposed to limit mobile ICBM deployments to no more than 1600 RVs carried on up to 800 delivery vehicles. The United States, which has plans of its own to deploy mobile ICBMs, appears willing to consider dropping its proposal to ban mobile ICBMs on the condition the Soviets will agree to (1) deployment practices and cooperative measures to assist in verifying the number of mobile ICBMs deployed and, possibly, (2) a sublimit regarding the types and numbers of mobile ICBMs deployed by each side.

---

* A major thrust of the 1983 *Report of the President's Commission on Strategic Forces* (the Scowcroft commission report) was to recommend that the United States deploy some MX missiles in order to encourage the Soviets to move toward the deployment of smaller, mobile ICBMs and, hence, foster a more stable balance—a proposition embraced by administration spokesmen. Now that the Soviets are doing this, the Reagan administration seems to be having second thoughts.

● *Verification*

It is widely agreed that the arrangements required to monitor compliance with the START treaty will need to be more extensive and intrusive than anything yet agreed upon by the superpowers, including the unprecedented verification measures set down in the INF treaty.* Numerous details remain to be worked out regarding methods for monitoring numerical limits on SLCMs, mobile ICBMs, and non-deployed missiles; the numbers, armaments, and range of ALCMs and SLCMs; and measures to assess ballistic missile throwweight.

● *ALCM parameters and counting rules.*

While both sides agree that long-range air-launched cruise missiles will be permitted and counted in the 6000 accountable weapons aggregate, important differences over ALCMs remain. Under SALT II, the superpowers agreed that all ALCMs with a range greater than 600 kilometers—whether they were nuclear- or conventionally armed—would be treated as nuclear-armed. Thus, any bombers carrying them were to be counted as strategic nuclear delivery vehicles within the SALT II treaty. In START the United States seeks to exclude completely long-range, conventionally armed ALCMs from the various limits.† Moreover, the United States proposes that even nuclear-armed ALCMs would have to have a range of greater than 1500 kilometers to count in START.

To ease verification requirements (and to provide some "discount" in charging ALCMs against the 6000 ceiling), the United States also proposes that an arbitrary attributed value of ten ALCMs be assigned for bombers equipped with nuclear-armed ALCMs, regardless of the actual number they may be able to carry. The Soviets have rejected the U.S. approach, insisting instead that all ALCMs with a range of more than 600 kilometers, whether conventionally or nuclear-armed, be counted in START. They also propose that ALCMs be counted according to the maximal number of missiles each ALCM-capable bomber is

---

* After insisting for decades that on-site inspection (OSI) represented little more than a Western scheme to permit intelligence collection inside Soviet territory, the Soviets under Gorbachev have proven willing to accept OSI measures for monitoring compliance with arms control treaties. In the case of the INF treaty, they have agreed, among other things, to OSI at INF missile operating bases and destruction and support facilities, and continuous monitoring of entry/exit portals at missile production facilities.

† Neither side deploys long-range conventionally armed ALCMs today.

equipped to carry. The Soviets have suggested, for example, that ALCM-equipped U.S. B-52s be charged twenty-eight accountable weapons, that B-1Bs be charged twenty-two, and that their Bear Hs be charged only six.

• *Limits on nondeployed missiles.*

Only RVs actually deployed in ICBM silos, on rail and road mobile launchers (if permitted), and aboard nuclear-powered, missile-carrying submarines are to be counted within START's 6000 ceiling. Likewise, only deployed missiles will count against the 1600 SNDV ceiling. Both sides have additional nondeployed missiles to serve as spares, for continuing flight-test programs and, in the Soviet case, for wartime reloads of their mobile and silo launchers. For example, at the time that the INF treaty came into force, the United States had on hand a total of 234 Pershing II missiles, only 108 of which were operationally deployed.[1] Both the United States and the Soviet Union have agreed in principle to limit nondeployed missiles under START, but they have not yet agreed on the size of this limit or on measures to monitor compliance.

Choices for the Next Administration

In addressing issues of strategic nuclear forces and arms control, the next administration will face a rather sharply constrained set of choices. We have noted that the basic START framework and the bulk of the drafting of detailed treaty language are already completed. Indeed, there is an outside chance that Ronald Reagan will sign a completed START treaty prior to January 1989, in which case "all" his successor would have to do is sell the treaty to the Senate and then live within its provisions.

Yet, aside from the question of who completes and signs the treaty, the ways in which the next administration shapes this country's strategic nuclear forces to conform to START's limits will help determine the viability of the U.S. strategic nuclear force posture through the end of this century and beyond.

In the remainder of this chapter, we assess the major choices that will confront the next administration with respect to these issues:

• Completing the START treaty (assuming that the issues reviewed above remain unresolved on inauguration day)
• The American strategic nuclear force structure within the START framework
• Strategic nuclear arms control beyond START.

Completing the Treaty

As noted above, the major stumbling block to completion of the START treaty remains the dispute between the United States and the Soviet Union over the proper interpretation of the ABM treaty. Potential resolutions of these differences, and the broader but related question of potential roles of ballistic missile defense in American security strategy, are reviewed in the next chapter. It is worth noting here, however, that the ways in which Ronald Reagan's successor handles the issue of SDI testing and development—within the context of both a treaty resolution and the nature and level of development and testing activity it actually undertakes—will have considerable bearing on the prospects for Senate ratification of the START treaty.

If the price for a START treaty is some agreed-upon limitations on the conduct of the SDI testing program, opponents of the treaty will surely argue that the president, whoever he may be, sold out Ronald Reagan's vision of a highly effective defense shield over the West in order to get an agreement with Moscow.* Protecting options for the testing of space-based ballistic missile defenses may, therefore, be more important politically than militarily.

Aside from the issue of linkage between START and SDI, how might the next administration seek to resolve the differences outlined above?

Verification Issues. The START treaty is certain to include provisions for monitoring compliance that go well beyond the rather modest cooperative measures specified in SALT II. The joint document issued by President Reagan and General Secretary Gorbachev at the conclusion of the Moscow summit stated that START verification measures will include "at a minimum" the following:

- Data exchanges and inspections to verify the accuracy of the data provided
- On-site observation of the elimination of strategic systems
- Continuous on-site monitoring of the perimeter and portals of critical production facilities
- Short-notice, on-site inspection of various facilities and the right to implement, in accordance with agreed-upon procedures, short-notice inspections at suspect sites

---

* Treaty opponents will find it considerably easier to make this argument if someone other than President Reagan signs the START treaty—a fact that surely has not escaped Moscow's notice.

- Provisions prohibiting the use of concealment or other activities that impede verification by national technical means (including a ban on telemetry encryption during missile test flights)*
- Procedures to enable verification of the number of warheads on deployed ballistic missiles
- Measures designed to enhance observation of treaty-related activities by national technical means.[2]

Agreement on this set of measures is in itself an impressive accomplishment. Significant further measures, however, remain on the negotiating agenda. Three issues seem to be particularly thorny: monitoring with high confidence numbers of mobile ICBMs and nondeployed ICBMs and SLBMs, distinguishing between conventionally armed and nuclear-armed SLCMs, and limiting the breakout potential inherent in the deployment of large numbers of conventionally armed, long-range cruise missiles.† As with the resolution of the interpretation of the ABM treaty, verification may be a crucial part of the ratification debate. These issues will therefore merit high-level attention.

Monitoring Mobile ICBMs. A host of measures for enhancing the ability of the United States to monitor numbers of mobile ICBMs have been proposed. These measures include the designation of bases and deployment areas outside of which mobile missiles normally could not travel, requirements for advance notification when movements of missiles outside of these areas is contemplated, short-notice inspections of individual deployment areas, and permanent portal monitoring of bases.

The purpose of designated bases and deployment areas is to make cheating more risky. Under an arms control regime in which one side claimed to have deployed, say, 500 missiles on mobile launchers, the monitoring nation would have to account for at least 501 deployed launchers all at once in order to show that the limit had been violated—a near impossibility. Under an arrangement that specified deployment

---

* Data transmitted from missile payloads to ground stations during test flights of strategic ballistic missiles (that is, telemetry data) have been an important source of information to each side on the capabilities of the other's nuclear-armed missiles. The Reagan administration has accused the Soviets of encrypting key portions of these data to deny them to U.S. intelligence analysts.

† "Breakout potential" here refers to the possibility of rapidly converting a missile's warhead from conventional to nuclear. This problem is not solely a verification issue, though measures to address it tend to focus on means to ensure compliance with declared numerical limits.

bases and areas, however, detection of just one unauthorized launcher outside such areas or one excess launcher within a particular base or area would document a violation. At a minimum, this arrangement would encourage a cheater to deploy his illegal missiles and launchers inside the deployment areas and thus allow the other side to focus its surveillance efforts on those areas.

Mobile missiles are survivable only if one's adversary cannot locate most of them precisely. Given this imperative, neither side is likely to permit the other to find a large portion of the missile launchers in any deployment area at one time. One way to enhance monitoring confidence would be for both sides to agree to display, in response to a short-notice request from the other side, all missile launchers at deployment bases within an individual deployment area, for observation by overhead surveillance. This might entail opening the roofs of all the garages housing mobile missile launchers and parking the launchers in front of them. Any mobile launchers that could not be so displayed (for example, those that had broken down in the field or were away from base for major maintenance) would have to be accounted for.

Any unaccounted-for missile launcher that was found within the deployment area and not at a deployment base during the inspection would constitute a violation. This provision would make the deployment of illegal missile launchers within a deployment area more risky. Limited on-site inspection provisions within deployment areas could add to both sides' confidence that launchers were not being concealed within those areas.

Because only one deployment area at a time would be subject to the display and inspection procedure, survivability of the mobile ICBM force as a whole would not be significantly jeopardized. Deployment areas could not be contiguous, so juggling among different areas missile launchers in excess of those allowed could be detected.

Collectively, these measures appear adequate to the task of monitoring the number of mobile missile launchers deployed by both sides. There is a potential downside to these measures, however. In its zeal to achieve a capability for high-confidence monitoring of mobile ICBMs, the United States must be careful not to prevent either side from deploying mobile ICBMs in survivable ways. Talk of confining mobile missiles to garrisons and very small deployment areas leads one to suspect that first-strike stability—the basic reason for deploying mobile missiles—may be sacrificed on the altar of verifiability.*

---

* The United States, for example, is said to have proposed that each side agree to restrict its mobile ICBMs to an area of ten square miles around each missile base.[3]

Monitoring Nondeployed Missiles. All of the measures outlined above are directed toward monitoring numbers of deployed missile launchers. They do not, for the most part, apply to monitoring missiles themselves, including stocks of nondeployed missiles.

The Soviets may have developed procedures for the rapid reload of ICBMs onto mobile missile launchers and into silos. In addition, design features of their latest generation of strategic missiles, including solid or storable liquid fuel and the capability for "cold launch," make these missiles well suited for reload operations or for possible launch without elaborate launch facilities. Conceivably, a number of ICBMs and launchers could be produced and stored for many years, then rapidly deployed in a crisis or even following the outbreak of nuclear war. A basic decision is needed, then, on whether to strive both for treaty provisions that would place strict limits on nondeployed missiles and for measures that would allow the United States to monitor their numbers with some confidence.

If nondeployed missiles are to be counted, some sort of inventory control system will be needed. Such a system might include portal monitoring and challenge inspection procedures of the types mentioned above. These procedures, similar to those agreed on under the INF treaty, would allow both sides to have reasonable confidence in their estimate of the number of missiles produced once the treaty's monitoring regime was in place. They would not, however, address the problem of verifying the number of missiles claimed to exist prior to that time.

A missile inventory and tagging system would be useful in helping to deal with this problem, as well as in keeping track of deployed mobile ICBMs and launchers. Both sides have already agreed to declare their full inventories of strategic missiles existing at the time of START's ratification. They might also agree to allow the other side to install tamper-evident serial number tags on each declared missile and on all missiles produced thereafter. After a certain grace period (say, 180 days), any strategic missile without a tag or with a duplicate numbered (counterfeit) tag would constitute a violation.

This provision, coupled with that for challenge inspections at declared missile support facilities and possibly at nondeclared sites where missiles might be stored covertly, would help to deter the retention of nondeclared missiles. Moreover, monitoring of portals at centralized missile maintenance facilities would make it impossible to maintain such missiles without elaborate deception measures and substantial risk of detection.

ALCMs. Resolving the issue of how to account for nuclear-armed ALCMs under START appears to be straightforward. The two sides should agree to attribute to each bomber type capable of launching nuclear-armed ALCMs a more-or-less notional carriage capacity. Multiplying this attributed value by the number of bombers of that type would yield the charge to be levied against the 6000 ceiling. A more rigorous approach—counting and tagging actual ALCM inventories— seems excessively elaborate for this purpose. The only issue, then, becomes what the attributed number should be for each type of bomber. The number chosen should be reasonably close to the average number of ALCMs carried by each type of bomber under operational conditions.* No doubt the two sides will be able to settle this issue to their satisfaction.

What to do about conventionally armed, long-range ALCMs may be a more difficult question to resolve. The United States wants to protect the option to deploy a sizable number of such missiles. According to press reports, these missiles will be about as large as the AGM-86B— the currently deployed U.S. nuclear-armed ALCM. Deployment of large numbers of conventionally armed missiles creates a potential for breaking out of treaty limits, should the deploying country choose to substitute a nuclear warhead for the conventional one.

U.S. efforts at Geneva (so far unsuccessful) to raise the range threshold for nuclear ALCMs have been aimed, in part, at resolving this problem. Conventionally armed ALCMs would have considerably less range than nuclear-armed ones of comparable size because of the greater weight of conventional warheads. But this means that adjusting the range threshold to fall between those of the nuclear and the conventional ALCMs cannot by itself reduce the breakout potential associated with large conventionally armed ALCMs, since their range presumably would increase if their warheads were exchanged for lighter, nuclear ones.

It has to date been deemed infeasible and undesirable, at least in official U.S. circles, to seek arms control agreements that limit the number and type of nuclear warheads or fissile materials produced. In the absence of such limits, breakout potential would have to be limited by ensuring that missiles declared to be conventionally armed were constructed in such a way as to make it difficult for them to accommo-

---

* ALCMs, like penetrating bombers, are subject to interception by air defense fighters and surface-to-air missiles. It seems reasonable, therefore, to apply a modest discounting factor to the carriage capability of ALCM-capable bombers.

date a nuclear warhead. It may well be that the design of both sides' missiles today essentially precludes rapid convertibility. It seems unlikely, however, that either side would be prepared to allow the other to examine the innards of its missiles in order to be assured of this.

Another approach might be to "lock in" the warheads of conventionally armed ALCMs with devices that would disable the missile in the event the warhead was covertly removed. Such devices would have to have two "keys" (actually alphanumeric codes), one held by each superpower. Personnel from both sides could release the lock when it was necessary to remove a warhead for maintenance or other purposes, and reinstall it when the procedure was completed. Such an arrangement, while effective, would be rather awkward and expensive. Alternatively, it might be possible to devise functionally related observable differences (FRODs) that would allow each side to distinguish the other's nuclear ALCMs from conventional ones by an external inspection.

A simpler approach seems feasible. The U.S. conventionally armed ALCMs will be associated with a limited number of dedicated delivery vehicles (initially fewer than 100 B-52Gs). By removing from these platforms the avionics and wiring needed to arm nuclear weapons, and taking other steps to denuclearize them, such as eliminating nuclear weapons storage areas from their bases, the United States could make the case that these aircraft were not operationally capable of delivering nuclear weapons, and thus should not count against START limits.*

The advantage of this approach is that monitoring efforts could focus on ensuring that a relatively small number of bombers (and not the hundreds or even thousands of conventionally armed ALCMs to be procured) were not converted for nuclear weapons carriage. This would, of course, entail the use of challenge inspections at several bomber bases to verify the nonnuclear character of these platforms. If the Soviets demurred from wholly excluding these bombers from START totals, the United States might be able to accept a provision whereby each nonnuclear B-52 might count only one against the 6000 and 1600 limits.

SLCMs. The Soviets' insistence on tight controls on the number of nuclear-armed SLCMs deployed presents a different and more intractable problem. The United States, at least, plans to deploy hundreds of

---

* Before proposing such an approach, the administration would need to satisfy itself that it would be prepared to accept the same provisions should the Soviet Union claim to deploy a force of conventionally armed heavy bombers.

nuclear-armed SLCMs and thousands of conventionally armed SLCMs and launchers on a wide variety of platforms, often deploying both types of missile on the same platform. The Soviet Union has developed two types of SLCM, one of which they began to deploy on submarines early in 1988. While the American plan for deploying mixed loads of nuclear and conventional SLCMs on a wide variety of platforms may have operational utility, it also makes infeasible the use of an approach based on a counting rule similar to that suggested for ALCMs.*

In December 1986, the Soviets claimed to have developed a gamma ray sensing device that can detect and assess the aggregate yield of nuclear weapons aboard even a nuclear-powered naval vessel without having to board it. Theoretically, such a device could be used to monitor numbers of deployed SLCMs. U.S. technical experts are skeptical, however, that a reliable means for remote sensing exists. Moreover, even if one could be devised, such an approach to monitoring nuclear SLCM deployments could jeopardize the U.S. Navy's long-standing policy of refusing to confirm or deny the presence of nuclear weapons aboard its ships, perhaps posing unacceptable risks for the navy's continued access to port facilities.

An effective monitoring regime for SLCMs, in short, might have to be based on a comprehensive inventory control system similar to one for keeping tabs on nondeployed ballistic missiles (that is, one based on the use of tags and on-site inspections).

Additionally, as with ALCMs, the United States and the Soviet Union each might want to assure itself that the other side could not rapidly or covertly convert its large force of conventionally armed SLCMs to nuclear weapons by changing the warheads and arming devices on each missile. Here again, because of the nature of U.S. deployment plans for SLCMs, restricting conventionally armed missiles to denuclearized platforms seems infeasible. If it is deemed imperative to eliminate this breakout threat, the dual-key approach described above would seem necessary.

Of course, if both sides were content simply to prevent the *covert* conversion from conventional to nuclear SLCMs, they could agree to place simple tamper-evident but nondestructive locks on the canisters of conventionally armed SLCMs at the factory. If the canister were opened, the other could detect this in random inspections.

---

* The Reagan administration rejected a suggestion, reportedly made by Ambassador Paul Nitze, that the United States revise its plans and deploy nuclear-armed SLCMs only aboard a small number of dedicated nuclear platforms. The following administration may wish to revisit this proposal.

In summary, the next administration will have three broad choices with respect to meeting Soviet demands for a limit on SLCMs:*

- A minimal, declaratory approach under which the United States and the Soviet Union periodically exchange information on their nuclear SLCM deployment programs.†
- Revising deployment plans for nuclear-armed SLCMs and agreeing to restrict their deployment to a small number of platforms and classes of vessels. This option would permit the use of an attributed value/counting rule approach to calculate the number deployed, although challenge inspections of ships claimed to be free of nuclear SLCMs would seem to be necessary.
- Comprehensive inventory control, using production monitoring, tagging, and challenge inspections. If controls on the conversion of conventional SLCMs were desired, dual-key locks would also be necessary.

Even this last, most ambitious, option could not assure that one side or the other had not retained a small number of nuclear-armed SLCMs in excess of those declared. But cheating on SLCM limits would be far less significant if both sides were permitted to deploy some of these weapons than if a total ban were in place. Nuclear-armed SLCMs pose a unique threat by providing each side with a capability for a small-scale surprise precursor attack on high-value assets, such as bomber bases and command and control nodes. Because they are so small and can be launched from unpredictable points offshore, SLCMs in flight can be very difficult to detect. Once a low threshold of SLCM deployments is crossed (say, a few dozen weapons, which would be sufficient to destroy all of the bomber bases and major command and control centers in the United States), the magnitude of this threat is quite independent of the number of SLCMs deployed. Given that the United States could not be confident of Soviet compliance with a ban on nuclear SLCMs, therefore, the actual level of the SLCM ceiling is

---

* A fourth alternative, banning nuclear SLCMs, seems infeasible even if it were deemed desirable: No measures to monitor warhead stockpiles are foreseen within START, and it would be nearly impossible to ensure that the Soviets had not covertly retained a small number of SLCMs with nuclear warheads to be employed in wartime.

† This appears to be the approach currently favored by the Reagan administration. Since these declarations would be statements of national policy and outside the treaty's obligations, they would not be subject to agreed-upon verification measures.

relatively unimportant, as is the need for comprehensive monitoring provisions to verify compliance with the ceiling.

In light of all these considerations, the solution currently favored by the Reagan administration—a simple declaratory approach—seems to be the best available, provided, of course, that the Soviets can be persuaded to go along.

Verification, Uncertainty, and Security

Many observers will regard measures such as comprehensive inventory controls and dual-key locks as unnecessarily elaborate. In their judgment, the military and political consequences of a treaty breakout based on SLCM conversion, covert deployment of missiles, and so forth, are not impressive. After all, in a world where each superpower deploys about 9000 strategic nuclear weapons, if the Soviets were to quickly deploy even one or two thousand additional warheads, they would not significantly alter the deterrent balance, particularly if such a breakout were overt or detected. In such a case, the United States could very quickly upgrade the alert status of all or some of its strategic forces (for example, by putting rail-mobile MX missiles out of their garrisons or placing a larger portion of its bomber force on alert), thereby at least partially compensating for any added threat to the survivability of its forces. Meanwhile, the United States could implement other, longer-term compensatory measures, such as deployments of additional launchers.

Moreover, the major assumption behind demands for treaty provisions to eliminate breakout options—namely, that such options exist only because of arms control—is false. If there were no arms control regime covering strategic nuclear weapons, either the United States or the Soviet Union could attempt a rapid or covert deployment of additional weapons. Indeed, in the absence of cooperative monitoring arrangements in a nontreaty regime, it would be easier to do so.

Those who express concern about the inability of the arms control process to govern every aspect of the strategic balance forget that arms control—at least on the model of START—is designed to operate more or less at the margins of the strategic balance. The goal of START is not, and should not be, to impose absolute equality and stasis on the strategic forces of both sides. Rather, it is to place an effective cap on the forces, as measured in rather gross dimensions. Unilateral measures to alter force structure and posture, such as new basing modes and adjusted alert rates, are likely to have a greater impact on survivability and first-strike stability than the bilateral reductions START would mandate.

START, then, cannot be a substitute for continued attention to the survivability and effectiveness of U.S. strategic nuclear forces. Nor can it be a source of great risk to U.S. security unless Americans mistakenly view it as a panacea.

Reopening Settled Issues?

Ronald Reagan's successor will likely have to decide how to pursue agreement on all or most of the issues mentioned above. In addition, of course, he will have the option of trying to change parts of the START draft treaty already agreed upon. Since the new president will have to both lead the fight for START's ratification and shape U.S. strategic nuclear forces to conform to the treaty's limits, he will want to be satisfied, on balance, with all of the treaty's provisions. This may lead him to reopen some areas of the treaty now settled.

There is a potential cost associated with this. The next president may be wary of beginning a process of renegotiation for fear that it could get out of control, leading to the unraveling of large portions of the treaty. In early 1977, for example, had President Carter been able to foresee that his effort to negotiate a radically new arms control treaty would result in a one- or two-year delay in the SALT process, he might have settled instead for the more modest SALT II treaty that he eventually got—a treaty based heavily on the 1974 Vladivostok accord, handed him by his predecessor, President Ford. Given the enthusiasm for nuclear arms control demonstrated by the current leadership in the Kremlin, such a scenario seems unlikely today. Nevertheless, conditions can change and the best can be the enemy of the good.

The basic framework of the START treaty is sound: The treaty provides for effective constraints on the destructive power of both sides' ballistic missile forces in particular. At the same time, it permits the United States sufficient flexibility with which to structure a survivable, effective, and affordable triad of strategic nuclear forces, as we shall see below. Still, the next administration could probably reopen at least minor provisions of the treaty without undue risk.

One element of the current draft treaty deserving of particular scrutiny is the ceiling of 1600 it would place on SNDVs. As has already been noted, this ceiling could discourage efforts to proliferate aim-points and strengthen first-strike stability through the deployment of sizable numbers of single- or two-RV ICBMs. Since warheads and throwweight are the basic units of account in START, raising the SNDV ceiling to, say, 1800 or 2000 need not result in an increased level of deployed destructive capacity. Nor should the Soviets be expected to offer much resistance to such a revision, given their evident determination to maintain a viable ICBM force.

There is one potential objection to this change. Heavy bombers not equipped to carry ALCMs will count only one against both the weapons and the SNDV ceilings, although each bomber can carry perhaps sixteen short-range missile or gravity bombs. Theoretically, if the SNDV ceiling were raised, either side would be able to deploy a huge bomber force with many thousands of weapons while remaining technically in compliance with both START ceilings. Therefore, if the United States wishes to push for a higher SNDV ceiling, it may have to be prepared to accept at least a nominal ceiling of, say, 350–400 on nuclear-capable heavy bombers.

Additional Measures?

At the beginning of this chapter we noted that arms control agreements can reduce attack potential not only by eliminating forces but also by restricting the development or deployment of certain capabilities that might pose a special threat to force survivability. SALT II, for example, provided for a ban on systems that would permit the rapid reloading of ICBM launchers. It also prohibited the development, testing, and deployment of fractional orbital missiles and long-range missiles emplaced in the seabed or on surface ships. Accordingly, the next administration might want to consider including additional measures in the START treaty that have not, to date, been addressed in the negotiations.

Banning Depressed-Trajectory Flight Tests. One restriction that might usefully be incorporated into the START treaty is a ban on the testing of strategic ballistic missiles, particularly SLBMs, in depressed-trajectory flights. Unlike a normal, "minimum-energy" trajectory, in which a missile's payload is lofted in a high arc toward its target, a depressed trajectory would deliver weapons to target at a higher average speed and along a lower arc. While some range and accuracy would be sacrificed, a depressed-trajectory flight would allow a missile to reach its target in a fraction of the time needed with a minimum-energy trajectory.

To illustrate the threat posed by depressed-trajectory attacks, let us consider an attack by Soviet SLBMs on U.S. bomber bases. Using a minimum-energy trajectory, a missile launched from the central Atlantic coast would require approximately fifteen minutes to reach McConnell Air Force Base in Kansas, about 1000 miles away. This should be sufficient time for the B-1 bombers on alert there to launch and fly far enough from the base to escape the blast of several warheads. If a depressed-trajectory attack were employed, however, the missile's flight time could be cut to around eight minutes. This reduction in warning time might well be sufficient to preclude the launch of alert bombers. Airborne command and control posts and, in the future, mobile ICBMs whose survival was based on a "dash on warning" concept would also be endangered by depressed-trajectory attacks.

Fortunately, neither the United States nor the Soviet Union has tested missiles in a depressed-trajectory mode (at least insofar as is publicly known). It would seem useful, therefore, to proscribe such tests now, in order to prevent the eventual emergence of this capability. Of course, such an agreement need not be part of the START treaty. A mutual pledge to forgo testing of missiles in a depressed-trajectory mode could probably be readily formalized in an executive agreement. But since banning these tests seems useful and noncontroversial, as well as being inherently related to the content and purposes of a START treaty, including the ban in START would modestly increase the treaty's value and, presumably, its prospects for ratification.

Sanctuaries for Ballistic Missile Submarines (SSBNs). Some proponents of arms control in both the United States and the Soviet Union have advocated the creation of sanctuaries for SSBNs as a means of enhancing the survivability of this leg of the triad.[4] These sanctuaries would consist of large areas designated in the open seas and, perhaps, around the territorial waters of the two superpowers; each superpower would refrain from employing specialized antisubmarine warfare (ASW) forces—aircraft, surface vessels, and hunter-killer submarines (SSNs) in the other's sanctuary zones. These ASW forces could, of course, be employed in one's own sanctuaries, where they would provide the primary means of monitoring compliance with the sanctuary agreement.

The advantages and disadvantages of ASW sanctuaries present a more mixed picture than those associated with banning depressed trajectories. SSBNs at sea seem quite survivable today. And not all threats to SSBNs would be neutralized by sanctuaries. Undersea acoustical sensors, for example, might continue to track SSBNs within the sanctuaries. Space-based sea surveillance capabilities would likewise be unaffected.

More importantly, the U.S. Navy has long opposed the idea of ASW sanctuaries, claiming that they would impose unacceptable restrictions on its global operations. To be useful, the sanctuaries would have to be quite large, each covering thousands of square miles of ocean. Prohibiting the navy from operating ASW forces in these waters would be tantamount to prohibiting any sizable naval operations there, since naval task forces always include substantial ASW support for hunting not SSBNs but SSNs that might threaten surface vessels. This may account in large measure for the Soviet Union's support for the idea of sanctuaries. The Soviets would undoubtedly like to blunt the navy's capability to operate near Soviet coasts—particularly in the SSBN bastions they have sought to establish in the Barents Sea and the Sea of Okhotsk.

Thus, while some form of SSBN sanctuary seems worthy of examination, the concept appears to have substantial risks and is certain to generate controversy and opposition in the United States. It would seem unwise, therefore, to push for provisions within the START treaty to create such zones.

Force Structure Choices

The overall impact of START on U.S. and Soviet strategic forces was shown in Figures 1 and 2. However, the treaty specifies only a rough structure of forces within its limits. Each side will have broad latitude in defining its START-compliant forces. In this section we examine the range of choices open to President Reagan's successor as he molds U.S. strategic forces to conform to the START treaty's limits. We also examine some of the major implications of those choices for U.S. national security.

The Bomber Force. Assuming that the next administration will wish to retain a relatively balanced triad of SLBMs, ICBMs, and bombers, a range of interesting choices exists for structuring its forces within START (see Figure 3). Determining the size of the U.S. bomber force deployed under START is relatively straightforward. The existence of a sub-ceiling of 4900 on ballistic missile RVs means that the United States would likely wish to deploy about 1000 accountable ALCMs—by the mid-1990s, a force consisting entirely of the low-observable advanced cruise missile (ACM). In addition, the United States would very likely deploy a sizable number of non-ALCM bombers in order to exploit the generous discount granted such platforms in charging their weapons against the 6000 limit.

Thus, if each B-52 equipped to carry nuclear armed ALCMs is charged twelve weapons, the United States might deploy eighty-four such ALCM carriers, plus its ninety-nine B-1Bs as penetrating bombers. By the mid-1990s, 132 B-2 (Stealth) bombers are scheduled to be operational as well, fully replacing B-52s in the penetrating bomber

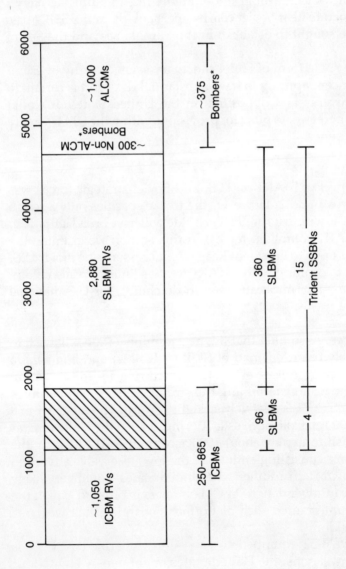

FIG. 3. *Alternative Force Structures Under START*

* includes 60 bombers for conventional missions

44

role. Finally, the United States might be compelled to count any dedicated, nonnuclear heavy bombers as one weapon against the 6000 ceiling and one SNDV against the 1600 ceiling. Assuming this is the case, the United States might deploy sixty such aircraft, for a total bomber force of 376 aircraft carrying 1300 accountable nuclear weapons and approximately 4700 actual nuclear weapons.

Of course, it is by no means certain that the United States will, in fact, deploy a sizable number of B-2s. The extremely high cost of these sophisticated aircraft—approximately $500 million apiece—will suffice to ensure that the program receives detailed scrutiny before a production decision is made.

Bombers and cruise missiles—so-called air-breathing systems—make an invaluable contribution to the resiliency of the triad by providing a hedge against the possibility that U.S. ballistic missiles may one day be unexpectedly rendered ineffective. But ALCMs and SLCMs can provide this hedge at a fraction of the cost of penetrating bombers.*

Penetrating bombers have long been advocated as platforms for attacking targets whose status or location is unknown. It is beyond the scope of this book to assess either the importance of this capability to U.S. strategy or the B-2's ability to provide it. However, several factors relevant to the acquisition of the B-2 should be noted:

- It appears that, for a relatively modest investment, the B-1B can be made to perform adequately as a penetrating nuclear bomber through the 1990s, at least in cases where a sizable number of ballistic missile weapons are allocated to suppressing Soviet air defenses.†
- The ACM, which can be carried by the B-52, will embody low-observable (stealth) characteristics that can stress existing and projected Soviet air defenses.
- The B-52 will not be able to perform the demanding low altitude penetration mission for many more years. Thus, if the United States does not procure a sizable number of B-2 bombers, it will not be able to take advantage of the generous discount accorded to weapons carried by penetrating bombers. Should the United States deploy no

---

* By one estimate, the United States can procure some 1700 stealthy advanced cruise missiles at a cost per weapon of just over $4 million. The cost per weapon deployed on a fleet of B-2 bombers is projected to be eight or nine times that figure.[5]

† Estimates of the cost to improve the B-1B's avionics to increase its survivability and effectiveness range from approximately $3 billion to $5 billion over five years.[6]

B-2s, its strategic nuclear forces under START would carry approximately 7200 weapons, as opposed to approximately 8600 on a force that included 132 B-2s.

Whatever the next administration (or *its* successor) decides about the B-2, it appears certain that the U.S. bomber and ALCM force will constitute between 1200 and 1300 accountable weapons against START's 6000 ceiling. Thus, there would be room for around 4700–4800 ballistic missile RVs in the U.S. force. The discussion that follows assumes that the United States can deploy no more than 4700 RVs.

SLBMs: Are Seventeen Tridents Enough? If ICBM and SLBM warheads were reduced by equal proportions (approximately 40 percent each) from their current levels, and if there were no changes in the size or loading of the Trident SSBN and its missiles, the U.S. force under START in the mid-1990s would include 3264 SLBM RVs on seventeen Trident boats and 1436 ICBM RVs on an as yet undetermined number of land-based missiles.

Of course, the portions of the U.S. triad presently given over to ICBMs and SLBMs are not sacred. They are the result of an accretion of separate programs and decisions that have shaped this country's strategic nuclear force structure over the past three decades. A lively debate has already begun on the subject of the future apportionment of warheads between ICBMs and SLBMs.

Much of this debate has focused on the size of the SSBN force. Put most crudely, the question is asked: "Are seventeen (or eighteen, or twenty) Trident boats enough?" The answer depends largely on whether and to what degree the survivability of the overall SSBN force is dependent upon the number of boats the United States deploys.

Today, the United States deploys twenty-six Poseidon and eight Trident SSBNs. These boats are rightly viewed as constituting the most survivable leg of the strategic triad of bombers, ICBMs, and SLBMs. Thus, the prospect of significant reductions in their numbers makes people uneasy. How should the United States shape its SSBN force to conform with the constraints of the START treaty?

Let it first be noted that by 1999, according to Congressional Budget Office documents, the navy plans to have retired all of the Poseidon SSBNs, replacing them with a total of only twenty Tridents even in an unconstrained, "no arms control" environment.[7] So START should not be held responsible for the lion's share of any projected reduction in the size of the U.S. SSBN fleet between now and the mid-1990s. Given a total force of seventeen boats, fifteen could be expected to be on-line on any given day.* Of these, ten would be to sea under normal conditions. Would twelve boats at sea day to day (the average number associated with a total deployment of twenty boats) offer appreciably more survivability? Would fifteen? It depends largely on the nature of the Soviet antisubmarine warfare threat today and the probable nature of any future breakthroughs in Soviet submarine detection capabilities—issues beyond the scope of this book.

The next administration will face a basic choice regarding the size of the U.S. SSBN force: If it believes that force survivability would be significantly enhanced by having more boats at sea, more Tridents could be deployed within a START agreement, either at the expense of the ICBM and ALCM forces or by reconfiguring the submarines or the missiles they carry. Deploying nineteen Tridents as presently configured, for example, while retaining the bomber force described above would reduce the permitted ICBM force to 1100 RVs. Alternatively, perhaps 6–8 of the twenty-four missile tubes on new Trident boats could be "filled in" with ballast, additional equipment and living quarters, or non-weapons-related launch vehicles.† Filling in eight tubes each on what might have been the last six boats under START, that is, boats 12 through 17, would allow the United States to deploy three additional boats for a total of twenty with the same 3264 RVs, albeit at substantial additional cost (around $2 billion per boat).

Alternatively, one could "download" Trident missiles, reducing the number of RVs deployed on each from eight to six. This would result in Trident boats each carrying 144 RVs instead of the 192 they carry today. A force of twenty-two such boats, then, would carry 3168 RVs, leaving, in our example, 1593 weapons for the ICBM force. Lightening the

---

* Submarines not in overhaul or in postoverhaul shakedown periods are considered to be on-line. It has been suggested that the START treaty include a provision exempting up to two SSBNs from counting against treaty limits, provided they are in dry dock with their missiles removed and the missile tubes somehow disabled. While this measure obviously would allow both sides to deploy more boats than would otherwise be the case, it would also permit a potential attacker, with careful planning, to augment his deployed forces rapidly by putting the two boats at sea to a breakout scenario.

† It has been proposed, for instance, that additional communications or reconnaissance satellites be deployed on missiles aboard Trident II submarines for rapid replacement of satellites that might be destroyed in wartime. The agreement announced at the Washington summit that the United States and the Soviet Union would verify the number of RVs on each missile type by on-site inspection would seem to make such deployments feasible without charging either the missiles or "phantom RVs" against START ceilings.

load carried by each Trident missile would have the added advantage of increasing the missile's effective range, thus enlarging the patrol area available to the Trident force and increasing its survivability.

There is a potentially serious downside of widespread missile downloading, however. Ballistic missile throwweight represents the best single measure of attack capacity. Thus, extensive downloading of ballistic missiles below their well-tested carriage capacity creates a serious breakout potential by permitting the maintenance of excess throwweight in the forces of both sides—throwweight that can be exploited by quickly reequipping missiles with their original RV loading. This problem emerged when the two sides agreed to accept each other's declarations of missile loading rather than rely on the SALT formula, under which missile loadings would be determined by the maximum number of RVs tested on the missile.* The Soviets then declared that their SS-N-23 SLBM will carry only four RVs even though it has been extensively flight-tested with 9–10. They have also declared the SS-18 ICBM a ten-RV missile even though the U.S. intelligence community believes it is capable of carrying as many as fourteen. While START will still impose significant and valuable reductions on Soviet ballistic missile throwweight, extensive downloading should be avoided in order to limit the remaining breakout potential.

The above discussion has addressed the question of how the United States can maintain a force of twenty or more SSBNs under START. It might, however, be the case that SSBN survivability is largely independent of the number of boats deployed, at least above a certain low threshold. In this case, all or some of the funds that would be needed to build the extra boats could be applied to other means of increasing SSBN survivability: research, development, and engineering aimed at further improving SSBN survivability through enhanced quieting and other signature reduction measures; deeper diving capability for SSBNs; procurement of more ASW capability; and so on. Careful study should be devoted to the question of which path—more boats or further improvements to the performance of boats—offers a better return for the dollar before the United States decides how to proceed with the SSBN modernization program.

Finally, it might be possible to build smaller SSBNs, carrying substantially fewer missiles and RVs than the current Trident boats, at lower cost. Given the lengthy lead times associated with the design,

---

* Both sides agreed in principle to accept monitoring provisions that will allow them periodically to inspect the payloads of ICBMs and SLBMs in order to verify compliance with these declared loadings.

testing, and construction of such craft, however, such an option would not be available for perhaps a decade.

Restructuring the ICBM Force. START represents a crossroads of sorts for the U.S. ICBM force. While START I cannot return us to the world of the 1960s, when ICBMs in silos were essentially invulnerable, it can help ensure the viability of a wide range of ICBM force mixes, most of which rely in part on mobility or redundant shelters. Of course, if reductions in the ICBM force are implemented unwisely, the contribution of this leg of the triad to national security could be significantly diminished.

Figure 4 illustrates the current ICBM force and three possible mid-1990s forces under START. Two characteristics are depicted: RVs and aimpoints.

The current American ICBM force deploys 2289 weapons on 1000 aimpoints. Each of these aimpoints is an underground silo. Recall that an even apportionment of reductions between ICBMs and SLBMs would leave 1436 RVs for the ICBM force. One way to adjust today's force to conform to START limits, while continuing to modernize the force, would be to retain the most modern and capable of the silo-based missiles—50 MXs and 152 Minuteman IIIs—and to add 48 MX missiles in a rail-garrison basing mode. (This is the notional force in Figure 4.) Under day-to-day conditions, this force would be based on fewer than 210 aimpoints. Given several hours to disperse the rail-garrison missiles onto the U.S. rail network, thousands of additional aimpoints would be generated.

But the United States has always called on its strategic forces to provide substantial survivability under day-to-day conditions as well. Going from an ICBM deployment pattern of 2.3 U.S. weapons per aimpoint today to almost 7 per aimpoint in the case of the notional force reduces substantially the price to attack imposed by the ICBM leg of the triad, even relative to the reductions in Soviet RVs imposed by START.* It is widely assumed that, should the Soviets contemplate a strike against U.S. ICBM silos, they would plan to allocate two warheads against each silo in order to attain a high probability of destroying it. Deploying the notional ICBM force would reduce the price to attack the entire ICBM force from 2000 weapons to 420 weapons.

This option should be avoided for two reasons: First, charging a smaller price to destroy our ICBMs (or at least their silos) may make a

---

* In this case, a 50 percent reduction in Soviet RVs would be accompanied by an 80 percent reduction in U.S. ICBM aimpoints. Put differently, the ratio of Soviet "hard target capable" RVs to U.S. ICBM aimpoints would increase from less than 4:1 today to 9:1.

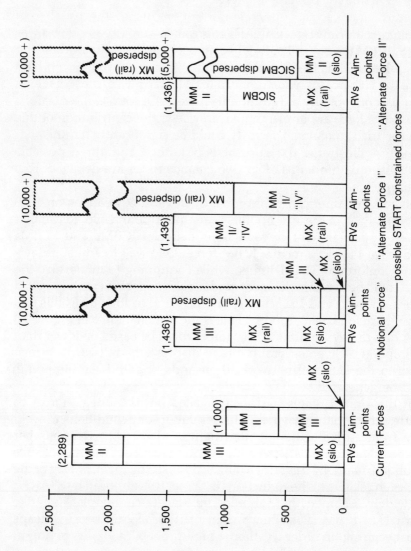

FIG. 4. *Current and Alternative START-Constrained ICBM Force Structures*

counterforce first strike more attractive simply by reducing the portion of the Soviet force required to perform the attack.

Second, and perhaps more important, reducing the number of aimpoints undermines a key attribute that has always pertained to ICBMs and bombers—namely, that they cannot be destroyed without unleashing a sizable nuclear attack on the territory of the United States. Although it may at first blush seem perverse to regard this as an advantage, the deterrent effect of such a force is much greater than that of a force that could be attacked without inflicting damage on the United States, since an aggressor might believe that attacking the "offshore" force would be unlikely to provoke a retaliation against his territory. In general, then, the smaller the number of strategic force aimpoints on U.S. soil, the more tempting a counterforce first strike might appear.

To illustrate, a counterforce attack of, say, 500 weapons that could effect a fundamental shift in the balance of forces may appear significantly less risky to the Soviets than one that would require more than 2000 weapons, as is the case today. The collateral damage associated with the former attack would be considerably smaller. In addition, today the Soviets might fear that U.S. attack assessment systems would not be able to distinguish between a 2000-weapon counterforce attack and a larger, full-scale attack that included targeting of U.S. urban-industrial assets, in which case an American president would have little reason to use restraint in ordering a retaliatory attack. In short, the smaller the "entry fee" for a counterforce attack, the greater the likelihood that such an attack might be seriously contemplated.

Accordingly, the next administration may want to structure its START-compliant ICBM force in ways that would offer more aimpoints than the notional force under day-to-day conditions. One way to do this would be to deploy the small ICBM (SICBM) on hardened mobile launchers (HMLs). A "maximal aimpoints" force incorporating 500 SICBMs on HMLs is shown in Figure 4 (alternative force II). In addition to the SICBM, this force combines 436 Minuteman IIs in silos with fifty MX deployed in a rail-garrison mode. Deployment of the SICBM in this mobile mode is expensive. Estimated procurement, operations, and maintenance costs for 500 SICBMs and an equal number of HMLs range upward of $40 billion. Costs for an equal number of RVs but on a two-RV version of the SICBM might be substantially lower. Note, however, that if the HMLs were deployed on Minuteman launch facilities, as is currently proposed, they would depend on tactical warning of an attack for the dispersal required to provide survivability.

Another approach to generating aimpoints would be to deploy the fifty MX ICBMs now in silos in a rail-garrison mode and retain 936 silos from today's Minuteman force. These silos could be filled with a combination of the 450 single-RV Minuteman II missiles deployed today and a new, single warhead version of the Minuteman that the air force has dubbed the Minuteman IV. The Minuteman IV, as envisaged, would retain the airframes and perhaps the guidance sets of the Minuteman III. If more aimpoints were desired, silos could be kept in excess of the number of missiles deployed (up to the current total of 1000), or additional silos could be constructed. In this case, the ICBMs could be deceptively placed among the silos in a way similar to the "shell game" scheme that was to be used for the MX and its multiple protective shelters.* While an "all silo" approach may be inferior in some ways to deploying SICBM, it represents a lower-cost alternative that assures a substantial price to attack under all scenarios, independent of tactical warning.†

START and First-Strike Stability. It will be recalled that an important objective of START is to strengthen (or, at a minimum, not weaken) first-strike stability. Reductions in force levels are themselves essentially neutral with respect to stability. They reduce both sides' attack potential, but also reduce numbers of retaliatory weapons. Whether these reductions' net effect on stability is positive or negative depends wholly on the nature of the forces deployed under START.

Figure 5 shows the number of U.S. and Soviet weapons that can exist both before an attack and at any point during an attack.‡ Here we have plotted the probable results of a hypothetical Soviet first strike against

---

* Using vertical silos would be substantially cheaper than the MX multiple protective shelter (MPS) basing scheme, which employed a large number of costly, horizontal shelters. Basing missiles in redundant silos would require special agreed-upon monitoring provisions. An attempt to negotiate such provisions could add to the time needed to complete a START treaty. Moreover, a multiple-silo basing scheme might face political hurdles in Congress because of residual prejudices regarding the checkered legacy of MX and its search for a suitable basing mode.

† This force, when combined with 408 Trident missiles (seventeen boats carrying twenty-four missiles each) and 376 bombers, exceeds by 170 the START ceiling of 1600 on SNDVs. As noted earlier, this ceiling is counterproductive with regard to first-strike stability because it discourages de-MIRVing and the proliferation of aimpoints. Consequently, the administration could try to renegotiate the ceiling or alter the ICBM force mix to fifty MX, 680 Minuteman II/IV, and eighty-five three-RV Minuteman III missiles.

‡ The authors are indebted to their colleague Glenn A. Kent for the mode of analysis employed here.

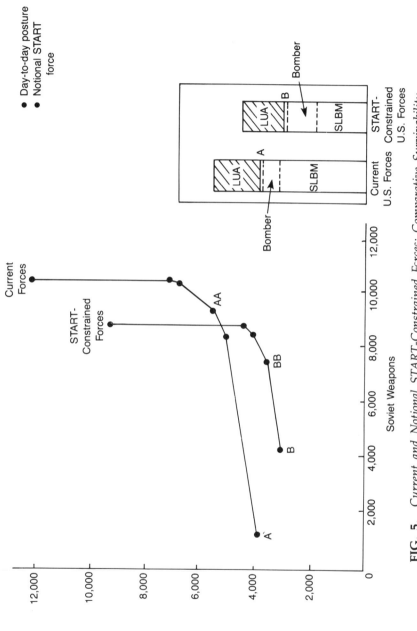

FIG. 5. *Current and Notional START-Constrained Forces: Comparative Survivability*

53

both current and START-constrained U.S. strategic nuclear forces under day-to-day alert conditions. (In this case, the notional U.S. force shown in Figure 4 was used. The appendix provides a breakdown of the assumed Soviet START forces, as well as the notional U.S. force.)

These curves show that START reductions can be expected to have a relatively minor impact on first-strike stability, at least over the near term. With respect to absolute numbers of weapons (stability I), should the United States deploy forces under START such as those in the notional force, and not raise alert rates for bombers or submarines, the survivability of its forces would decline somewhat relative to today's forces.

The northernmost point of each curve plots the pre-exchange balance of warheads. As the Soviets "spend" their weapons to destroy U.S. weapons, they move down along the curve until the Soviets run out of suitable counterforce weapons (at points A and B).* Surviving U.S. forces corresponding to these endpoints are shown in the bar graph section of Figure 5.

Under START, at least 3000 U.S. weapons could be expected to survive a Soviet first strike. If the United States launched its silo-based ICBMs out from under the attack (an outcome that the Soviets probably could not rule out), approximately 1300 more weapons would survive. These are depicted in the shaded area labeled "LUA" at the top of each bar.† Comparable figures for current forces are 4000 U.S. retaliatory weapons without LUA and an additional 1800 with LUA. In both cases, between one-third and one-half of the U.S. strategic forces would be expected to survive a first strike, depending on the number of silo-based ICBMs launched out from under the attack. In either case, the surviving weapons could do enormous damage to the Soviet Union in retaliation, assuming the Soviets had not deployed large-scale, effective ballistic missile defenses.

If the Soviets' objective in carrying out a first strike were to shift as much as possible the balance of strategic nuclear weapons (stability II), they would stop their attack at points AA and BB. Again, the notional U.S. START force with regard to this measure is marginally worse than

---

* The points depicted by the bar graph show the worst case from the U.S. perspective. In fact, a Soviet attack planner might choose to "stop" his attack at points AA and BB. Here, he has destroyed all U.S. SSBNs in port, all nonalert bombers, MX missiles in their rail garrisons, and most ICBM silos. To kill further weapons, he is forced to conduct inefficient barrage attacks against airborne bombers, expending 5–10 of his own weapons for each U.S. weapon destroyed.

† Weapons surviving as a result of launching out from under the attack are shown in the cross-hatched area labeled LUA for launch under attack.

the current force, assuming constant alert rates. Under current conditions, the ratio of Soviet to U.S. arms could shift from 1:1.15 to 1.75:1 (point AA). The notional START force would allow the Soviets the opportunity to shift the balance from around 1:1 to more than 2:1 (point BB).

That START alone is not responsible for this degradation in survivability is shown in Figure 6, where alternative force I is plotted alongside current forces. Point B is closer to point A than it was in Figure 5. This force is more survivable than the notional force. With alternate force I, at least 3300 U.S. weapons would be expected to survive a Soviet first strike. This improved result obtains because the single-RV silo-based ICBM force under alternative I imposes a considerably higher price to attack than do the ten- and three-RV forces of the notional force (1872 Soviet hard target kill RVs are required, as compared with 404). This high price, in turn, virtually eliminates the Soviet capability to barrage the flyout areas around U.S. bomber bases. Thus, more bombers survive a Soviet first strike. A similar result could be derived for the notional force by marginally raising the alert rates for U.S. bombers or, a more difficult proposition, for SSBNs.

A full analysis of first strike stability requires as well an examination of the survivability of Soviet forces. Drawdown curves are also useful for this analysis. For those not familiar with the two-sided drawdown format, Figure 7 shows the weapons domain in which the curves are plotted. The Soviet Union works to deploy its forces in ways that prevent the United States from being able to drive the Soviets' drawdown curve (S) into shaded area A. Likewise, the United States wants to avoid a situation in which the Soviets could drive its drawdown curve (U) into area B. Regions A and B encompass outcomes in which the side that initiates a war with a counterforce first strike is able to reduce its opponent's forces to very low levels relative to its own. If either or both sides achieve such a capability, both would feel strong pressures or incentives to undertake a first strike, especially in a crisis.

Figure 8 shows two illustrative pairs of drawdown curves, one stable, the other unstable. In the stable case (curves S and U), each side's forces impose a high price (denominated in weapons) to destroy them. Thus, the slopes of the curves quickly bend over, designating a poor exchange ratio. Neither side has much incentive (or pressure) to strike first.

In the unstable case (curves S' and U'), the price to attack each force is low. Thus, the side that strikes first can radically alter the balance of forces in its favor, perhaps even preventing an effective retaliatory attack.

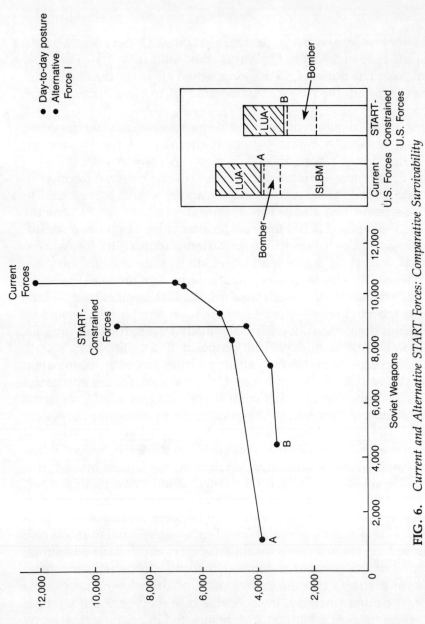

FIG. 6. Current and Alternative START Forces: Comparative Survivability

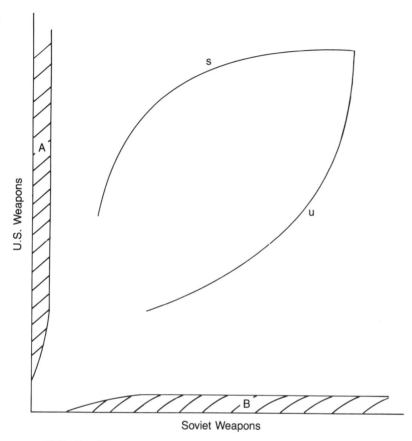

FIG. 7. *Weapons Domain for U.S. and Soviet Drawdown Curves*

Figure 9 adds two Soviet drawdown curves to the U.S. curves plotted in Figure 5. As has already been mentioned, the notional U.S. START force results in a relatively modest decrease in the number of U.S. weapons surviving a Soviet first strike (3000–4300 versus 000–5800). The Soviet drawdown curve under START, however, stops uncomfortably close to the vertical axis, indicating some potential for instability under this set of forces.

We obtain this result because assumptions regarding the day-to-day alert rates for Soviet strategic nuclear forces were carried over from current forces to mid-1990s START forces. In particular, the Soviets do not today keep any of their bombers on day-to-day alert. Such a practice would seem extremely unwise under the mid-1990s START force balance, since bomber-carried weapons will constitute both a larger absolute number and a larger share of Soviet strategic nuclear

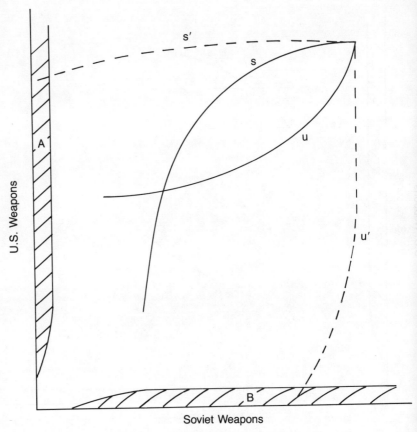

FIG. 8. *Notional Drawdown Curves*

weapons than they do now.* Should the Soviets wish to improve th
survivability of their day-to-day alert force under START, they cou
place a portion of these bombers on alert. They could also increase th
number of SSBNs and mobile ICBMs that they disperse out of the
ports and garrisons on a day-to-day basis.†

---

* The Soviet bomber force currently accounts for fewer than 1000 weapons c
of a total strategic nuclear force of more than 10000 weapons. We estimate th
by the mid-1990s, under START, Soviet heavy bombers will carry more th
4000 weapons out of a total of 9000.

† The Soviet Union has traditionally maintained only 15–20 percent of
ballistic missile submarines at sea on a day-to-day basis, as compared with
U.S. SSBN alert rate of around 60 percent. The portion of mobile SS-25 ICB
the Soviets maintain out of garrison on a regular basis, if any, is not publi
known.

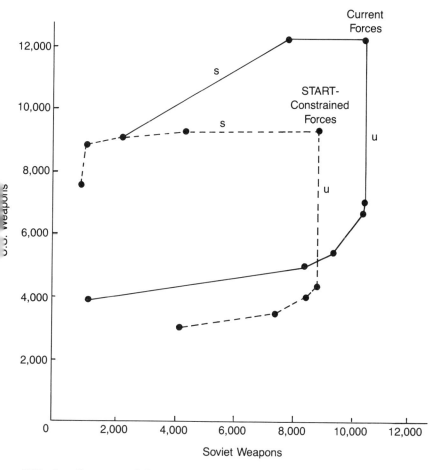

FIG. 9. *Current and START-Constrained Forces: Comparative Stability*

To summarize, START's chief contribution to first-strike stability is that it makes it easier to deploy forces in survivable ways by constraining the opponent's attack potential. A force of mobile ICBMs or de-MIRVed silo-based ICBMs that could be overwhelmed by a portion of an unconstrained Soviet force might be quite viable under a START-constrained regime. Likewise, the U.S. bomber force and, should the Soviets ever be able to determine the approximate location of the U.S. boats, SSBNs can be neutralized through barrage attacks if arsenals are permitted to grow large enough. START can prevent this from occurring. But, as the above analysis demonstrates, the problem of maintaining first-strike stability does not disappear when a START treaty is ratified. Continued attention to the survivability of U.S. forces will be as important as ever—indeed, perhaps more important than ever—under START.

How Much Is Enough?

Some critics of the START agreement will complain that, by reducing the number of weapons available to the United States, the treaty will "undermine deterrence" by correspondingly reducing the costs to the Soviets of a U.S. attack. The mode of analysis conventionally used to demonstrate the deterrent value of a given set of forces we call the thermometer exercise.

In a thermometer exercise, one posits a target base consisting of Soviet assets to be held at risk by U.S. strategic nuclear forces. These days, this base is said to consist of perhaps 9,000–10,000 targets, including Soviet strategic nuclear forces; ground, air, and naval forces for theater warfare; political and military leadership facilities; and economic and industrial assets.[8] A thermometer chart, or bar graph, is built with one bar for each category of target; U.S. weapons available in various scenarios are laid down on the target base, filling the thermometers to varying degrees. The higher the thermometers are filled, it is alleged, the greater the deterrence.

As Figures 5 and 6 showed, the most likely START forces will yield somewhat smaller retaliatory forces than those of today. If ongoing U.S. force modernization programs are carried to fruition, many of these weapons will be superior to those currently deployed in terms of both yield and accuracy. And START might reduce the size of the target base somewhat by reducing the number of aimpoints in the strategic nuclear forces category. Nevertheless, the smaller START forces would be expected to produce marginally lower "damage expectancies" in each thermometer. Does this, in fact, mean that deterrence is weakened?

Deterrence is based on the adversary's calculus of the potential gains, costs, and risks associated with aggression. Because this is a subjective judgment made by others (in this case, the Soviet leadership) and because it depends on so many factors beyond the number and effectiveness of U.S. weapons, no definitive answer can be given. Each individual will have his own intuitive feeling about where the threshold between adequacy and questionability lies.

As a point of reference, more than 25 percent of the population of the Soviet Union resides in that nation's 100 largest metropolitan areas.[9] A few nuclear weapons would be sufficient to destroy virtually all of the buildings in any of these cities. Our intuition tells us that the Soviet leadership is likely to view the prospect of being struck by at least

3000–4000 thermonuclear weapons as a thoroughly unacceptable consequence. Thus, with or without START, a deliberate, unprovoked nuclear attack on the United States would be all but inconceivable, and the Soviets would use a considerable degree of caution in considering provocative actions in areas of interest to the United States.

START II?

Washington and Moscow have yet to agree on the length of time during which the reductions to START-mandated levels would be implemented. The Soviet Union is said to favor a five-year period; the United States, seven years. In either case, the two nations will not have fully reduced to the ceilings specified in the treaty until after the end of the first term of the next administration. The United States will certainly want to gain some experience in living with START—particularly, in gauging the costs, risks, and benefits of the treaty's novel monitoring arrangements—before proceeding toward another round of reductions. It therefore would seem wise to concentrate post-START I negotiating efforts on the conclusion of a multinational treaty reducing conventional forces in Europe, the subject of chapter 4, postponing negotiations toward a START II treaty until the end of the first term or later.

Nevertheless, the next administration should begin promptly to think about how a second round of START could be formulated to strengthen U.S. security. The first question to be addressed seems to be: How low should we go? Further bilateral reductions in U.S. and Soviet nuclear forces to levels much below those imposed by START I are not obviously desirable. Reductions do diminish the already very low probability of an accidental or unauthorized release of a nuclear weapon simply by reducing the number of weapons in circulation. More significantly, however, very low levels of deployed forces also make the nuclear balance more sensitive to disruption because of cheating on arms control limits, technical breakthroughs, and other unforeseen developments.* Thus, safely reducing to much lower levels of forces could necessitate major and costly changes in force structure and posture to reduce vulnerability further.

The next president will have the opportunity (and obligation) to order a fresh look at the issue of how many strategic nuclear weapons

---

* The United States will want, in particular, to assure itself that strict and verifiable limits will continue to govern Soviet BMD capabilities before entering into a further round of reductions in offensive nuclear forces. The effects of such reductions on "extended deterrence," if any, will also have to be considered.

the United States must have to meet its security needs. The Soviets can be expected to continue exerting pressure on the United States and its allies to reduce and eventually eliminate nuclear weapons. In order to respond to Moscow's challenges in a coherent manner, the next administration must establish a broad consensus on the question of approximately how many nuclear weapons it needs.

We have already noted the inherently subjective nature of this problem. The analytical and political difficulties notwithstanding, it seems possible to provide a rational basis for an approximate force size. Conducting a review of U.S. nuclear weapon needs will require reopening the issues of what assets we wish to target and how many of each type must be held at risk in order to deter Soviet aggressiveness in areas of central importance to the United States.

Finally, independent of the outcome of this force sufficiency study, the next administration will want to keep in mind the possibility of future, deeper reductions under a START II agreement as it structures its forces under START I. Forces that appear to be optimal or acceptable under START I constraints may be quite inappropriate under a more ambitious arms control regime. For example, a START II agreement imposing a second "50 percent" reduction might put a ceiling of around 2500 on ballistic missile RVs. Clearly, in such a world, survivable forces with high day-to-day alert rates would be essential. More broadly, as forces get smaller, there will be less and less room in the force structure for elements that do not offer survivability and endurance under all plausible scenarios.

What general features might characterize desirable forces under such a regime? Highly MIRVed ballistic missiles in silos or on submarines would be much less attractive than they are today or even than they would be under START I, since they would concentrate the limited quota of ballistic missile RVs on a few platforms. Reducing the number of launch tubes on all Trident submarines or deploying smaller boats and de-MIRVed missiles (on the order of 50–75 RVs per boat, versus 192 today) would almost certainly be required if the United States were to continue to field an SSBN force of twenty or so boats.

A START II ceiling of 2500 on ballistic missile RVs could accommodate a de-MIRVed force of around 800–900 ICBM RVs deployed in a like number of silos. The price of attacking this force—1600–1800 RVs— would seriously tax the Soviets' total ballistic missile attack capability. If the United States wished to pursue this option, it could hardly afford to maintain a very large number of ten-RV MX missiles, either in silos or in a rail-garrison configuration.

Force planners on both sides presumably will be tempted to meet START II weapon constraints by downloading large existing missiles rather than undergoing further costly restructuring. The MX, for instance, might be reconfigured to carry six or four RVs instead of its current ten. This, however, would invite similar downloading of the Soviet SS-18 and SS-24 ICBMs. We have already noted the potentially serious impact of such cosmetic arms control on breakout potential. Accordingly, it might be useful under START II to contain this problem by specifying a ceiling on the amount of throwweight permitted on a missile for each RV it carries. If the ceiling were set at, say, 400 kilograms, a missile with 800 kilograms of throwweight would be counted as carrying two RVs. A missile with 850 kilograms of throwweight would be charged as carrying three RVs. Alternatively, the two sides might simply ban further downloading, returning, in effect, to the "maximum tested" rule of the SALT framework.

Summary

To summarize, we believe that the treaty emerging from the START negotiations can make positive and significant contributions to U.S. security. The treaty will strengthen arms race stability by increasing predictability regarding the evolution of both sides' forces and by placing comprehensive constraints on their overall attack capacity. By substantially reducing the Soviets' capacity for barrage attacks, START will also expand opportunities for the United States to deploy strategic nuclear forces in survivable ways. While adjustments imposed by the treaty have the potential to cause a modest near-term reduction in first-strike stability, this loss can be readily recouped, if necessary, by increasing bomber and submarine alert rates or by deploying ICBMs in a way that raises the price to attack them.

Our assessment of the issues remaining to be settled in the START negotiations has led us to the following conclusions:

- *The United States should abandon its position calling for a ban on mobile ICBMs.* Mobility is the most promising approach to increasing the survivability of ICBMs, and the Soviets are determined to pursue it (as should the United States).
- *ICBM survivability need not, and should not, be sacrificed in the interests of increasing confidence in the monitoring of mobile ICBM deployments.* It seems possible to devise a regime combining acceptable on-site inspection procedures and cooperative measures for enhancing the effectiveness of National Technical Means of verification (NTM) that would permit both sides to monitor deployments of mobile ICBMs

(as well as nondeployed missiles) without imposing harmful restrictions on their operations.

- *An acceptable means for monitoring numbers of deployed nuclear SLCMs does not appear feasible, given current deployment plans and practices.* While a complete ban on nuclear SLCMs might, on balance, be desirable, it could be circumvented with little cost or risk. And comprehensive monitoring of deployed SLCMs would impose unacceptable restrictions and risks on the U.S. Navy's operations. Thus, either the United States should hold out for a minimal, declaratory approach to keeping tabs on SLCMs, or it should plan to restrict the deployment of nuclear-armed SLCMs to a small number of dedicated platforms, thus making possible a counting rule approach. This would place a first-order constraint on numbers of deployed nuclear SLCMs. Procedures to constrain the conversion of conventional SLCMs to nuclear appear feasible but cumbersome and of limited utility.

- *The United States should retain the option to deploy long-range conventionally armed ALCMs without having to charge them against START limits.* At most, the next administration might accept a provision charging denuclearized heavy bombers as one against both the weapons and the SNDV ceilings of START. Both sides might supplement this approach by devising FRODs for their conventional (or nuclear) ALCMs.

- *The United States and the Soviet Union should consider raising the SNDV limit in the draft treaty from 1600 to 2000.* Raising the limit would protect potentially useful ICBM and SLBM deployment options aimed at de-MIRVing strategic nuclear forces. If the limit is raised, it would be advisable to place a nominal ceiling on the number of non-ALCM heavy bombers that either side could deploy.

- *Both sides should consider adding to the START treaty a provision banning flight tests of strategic ballistic missiles in a depressed-trajectory mode.*

We also have reached several conclusions relevant to the task of structuring U.S. strategic nuclear forces within the constraints of the START treaty. Primary among these is that unilateral decisions on the basing modes and alert posture of forces have a far more decisive impact than START-imposed reductions on survivability and first-strike stability. The corollary to this conclusion is that START can in no way substitute for modernization programs needed to maintain the survivability of strategic nuclear forces.

Other findings include these:

- *The United States should maintain a triad of ICBMs, SLBMs, and bombers.* The diversity of basing modes and delivery means offered by the triad provides a valuable hedge against unforeseen developments in the capabilities of both sides' offensive and defensive forces. Thus, the United States should deploy a sufficient number and quality of weapons in each element of the triad so that each can continue imposing a sizable attack price and present a substantial threat to Soviet assets.

- *The modernization of the ICBM force should have as its primary objective increasing the number of aimpoints presented by the force.* This may mean retaining or upgrading missiles that are less accurate than others such as the Minuteman II. Ideally, the attack price imposed by ICBMs (and other forces as well) should be independent of warning.

- *Increasing the number of SSBNs on patrol is not necessarily the best way to increase the survivability of the SLBM force.* Before choosing to build more Trident SSBNs and to reduce accordingly the number of RVs carried on each boat, the next administration should compare the marginal utility of such an approach with the utility of reducing further the signatures of U.S. SSBNs.

- *The next administration should begin early to explore the question of how far the United States can afford to reduce its strategic nuclear forces.* Very low levels of nuclear weapons will make it more difficult to maintain first-strike stability, to hedge against a breakout of treaty limits, and to pose credible threats of unacceptable damage to the Soviet Union. Nevertheless, further reductions beyond START I might be acceptable.

- *Decision-makers should keep in mind the possibility of future reductions below START I levels as they consider options for modernizing U.S. strategic forces.* Highly MIRVed missiles, which deploy large numbers of weapons on a single aimpoint, are particularly unattractive in the context of deeper reductions.

3

Defense and Space— The Future of the ABM Treaty

A MONG THE MOST important issues facing Ronald Reagan's successor are those related to the future role of strategic defenses in American security. President Reagan has brought the subjects of strategic defense in general and ballistic missile defense in particular to the forefront of the national security strategy debate after a period of more than a decade in which the prevailing offense-dominant nuclear weapons regime was taken as an immutable fact of life. His commitment to the idea of ballistic missile defense has spawned both the high-profile SDI and a controversial reinterpretation of the ABM treaty.

It is not only Moscow's insistence on linking the ABM treaty to START, then, that places this issue before the next president. With its multibillion-dollar-per-year SDI program, the Reagan administration has created anew a constituency for and broad interest in ballistic missile defense. At the same time, it has fostered considerable confusion about the scope and purposes of SDI and about the proper interpretation of the ABM treaty. Thus, one of the new president's first tasks likely will be to set a clear policy course for ballistic missile defense efforts in his administration.

Questions to be addressed by the new administration will include these: What is the correct interpretation of the ABM treaty? What clarifications of the treaty are necessary in light of new technological developments? What options for developing and deploying ballistic missile defenses should be protected and pursued, and at what level of funding? In short, what contribution can and should strategic defenses make to U.S. security in future years?

66

The Purposes of Constraints on Strategic Defenses

Like limits on offensive forces, constraints on the development, testing, and deployment of strategic defenses are intended to strengthen arms race, first-strike, and political stability. Since Hiroshima, we have lived in an offense-dominant world. That world is based on the enormous destructive power of nuclear weapons: An attacker can inflict catastrophic damage on his adversary even if only a small portion of his weapons reach their targets. The technical impossibility of effectively defending against a sizable nuclear attack, then, has been the basis upon which the United States and the Soviet Union have formulated their strategies for the posturing and employment of their strategic nuclear forces.

Some observers have made much of what they term the "doctrine" or the "strategy" of mutual assured destruction (MAD). In fact, MAD is neither a doctrine nor a strategy. Rather, it is a condition arising from the technical characteristics of nuclear weapons and their various delivery systems. This condition dictates, among other things, that both superpowers rely on threats of retaliation rather than on direct prevention of attack to protect their most fundamental security interests.

Given these conditions, in which the offense dominates, arms race and first-strike stability depend on constraining strategic defenses— especially wide-area defenses for the protection of the nation as a whole—to very low levels, while permitting offensive forces to be large, diversified, and highly survivable.* The ABM treaty has contributed to arms race stability by prohibiting an arms race in the deployment of BMD systems. (Under the treaty, each superpower may deploy no more than 100 ABM interceptor missiles at a single site.) The treaty also has dampened pressures for increases in offensive forces—increases that might otherwise have been deemed essential to maintain a capability to inflict unacceptable damage in the face of extensive but only partially effective ballistic missile defenses. By tying a completed START treaty to a resolution of the ABM treaty's interpretation, the Soviets have articulated a corollary to this proposition—namely, that the long-term acceptability of a treaty regime capping and reducing offensive strategic nuclear forces depends on a continuation of strict limits on strategic defenses (at least so long as either side wishes to maintain conditions of offense dominance).

Large-scale deployment of wide-area ballistic missile defenses can undermine first-strike stability in an offense-dominant world. While

---

* Point defenses for the protection of retaliatory forces may in some cases contribute to first-strike stability (see p. 76–77 below).

such defenses could be overcome in a large, well-structured first strike, they might be adequate to defend against a smaller, uncoordinated retaliatory attack. Returning to the drawdown curve format, Figure 10 overlays strategic defenses onto the offensive weapons domain. In this case, both sides are assumed to have deployed defenses capable of subtracting 5000 warheads from the other's attack. These defense potentials are displayed in the shaded areas (labeled A and B) along both axes.

In this world, neither side's defensive capability would be sufficient to preclude catastrophic damage from an attack that included substantially more than 5000 weapons. But if one side or the other could, in a first strike, draw its opponent's retaliatory weapons down to a level

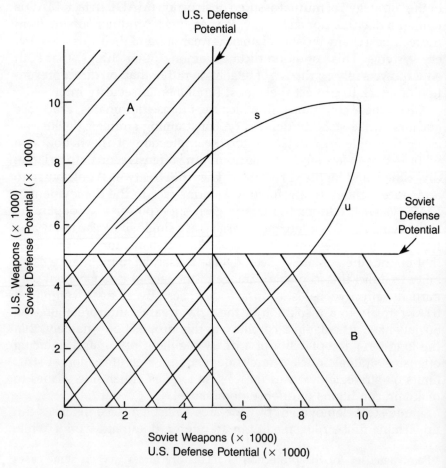

FIG. 10.   *Offense-Defense Interactions and First-Strike Stability*

below 5000, the attacker would have achieved, in conjunction with its defense potential, what Herman Kahn called a "splendid first-strike capability."*

Figure 10 depicts a situation in which both sides have achieved such a capability: By launching a first strike, the Soviet Union could draw down U.S. retaliatory weapons to a level that could be absorbed by Soviet defenses. The United States has a like capability. This world of mixed offensive and defensive forces yields a balance that might be termed mutual conditional survival (that is, either side's survival is assured on the condition that it strikes first). Such a mixed world would be highly unstable, since both sides would feel enormous incentives and pressures to initiate the use of nuclear weapons with a counter-force strike.

For reasons of both arms race and first-strike stability, then, the superpowers have recognized the desirability of effective bilateral constraints on the deployment of at least wide-area ballistic missile defenses until such time as they can agree to move toward a defense-dominant world. In such a world, conditions opposite from today's balance would be prescribed: Arms race and first-strike stability with respect to strategic nuclear forces would be based on limiting offensive forces to very low levels (perhaps down to zero), while permitting the deployment of extensive, survivable defenses against air and ballistic missile threats.

If it could be attained, such a world would offer a condition of mutual assured survival, as opposed to mutual assured destruction, but at a price: As we have noted, the West has long relied on nuclear weapons as a counterweight to sizable Soviet quantitative advantages in conventional ground and air forces around the periphery of the Soviet Union. Deterrence of aggression and intimidation by the Soviet Union against its neighbors in Central Europe, East Asia, and Southwest Asia continues to rest heavily on the perception that any conflict involving American and Soviet forces in these areas would carry an inherent risk of escalation to a nuclear exchange. It is far from clear how the United States would maintain deterrence in these areas in a world of mutual assured survival.

---

* This example assumes the deployment of nationwide, "random subtractive" defenses, such as might result from space-based interceptors. If a substantial portion of the defense potential had only limited-area coverage, an attacker with fewer than 5000 weapons might selectively overwhelm it in some places by concentrating attacks against a small number of targets.

Evolution of U.S. and Soviet Positions Since 1983

The evolution of U.S. and Soviet positions regarding research, development, and testing of ABM systems can be illustrated by reference to Figure 11. This chart shows the five basic phases of weapons development as applied to ballistic missile defenses. According to the longest-standing interpretation, the ABM treaty clearly permits activities in the first two steps of the stairway in this diagram (research and testing in laboratories), and it clearly prohibits activities in the last two (flight tests of components and actual deployment) if the ABM systems being tested are space-based, air-based, sea-based, or mobile land-based.

Activities in the third step (flight tests of subcomponents) are less clear-cut, since the distinction between a subcomponent and a component is ambiguous. Determinations regarding this distinction could be made on the basis of the power level or brightness (in the case of directed energy weapons), target engagement capability, and other technical characteristics of the piece of hardware being tested.

Soon after President Reagan gave his well-known "Star Wars" speech in March 1983, the Soviets began to demand measures that would kill the ambitious new U.S. BMD research program (later christened SDI). They initially called for a ban on all activities, including "scientific research," directed toward the development and eventual

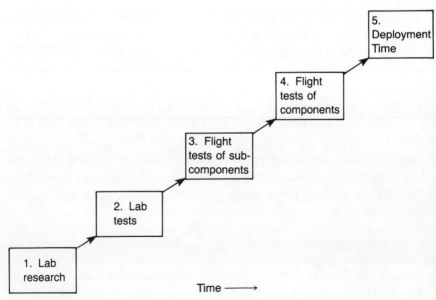

FIG. 11.　*Steps Toward the Deployment of Ballistic Missile Defenses*

deployment of space-based weapons. That is, they wanted to ban activities related to these weapons even within the first step of our diagram. This demand encompassed both BMD weapons and anti-satellite (ASAT) weapons based in space.

This position characterized Soviet proposals throughout 1984 and 1985. It would have ruled out virtually all U.S. research and development projects on advanced ballistic missile defenses, many of which predated the president's speech. At the same time, the Soviets' approach would have sanctioned most or all ongoing Soviet research on BMD because there is no public record documenting any Soviet intent to develop, test, or deploy defensive BMD or ASAT systems that are not fixed and ground-based. An agreement incorporating the Soviet position would have been virtually impossible to verify, since it would involve monitoring the purposes of research conducted in laboratories.

As the Soviets were trying to tighten drastically the strictures contained in the ABM treaty, the Reagan administration was pushing in the other direction. In the fall of 1985 the administration announced its new, "broad" interpretation of the ABM treaty, which would permit the unrestricted development of ABM systems based on "other physical principles," no matter how they were to be deployed.* All that would be prohibited, in this view, would be the actual deployment of operational weapons (step 5). Although the administration, under pressure from Congress, subsequently announced that for the time being the United States would abide by a "strict" interpretation of the treaty (actually, the traditional interpretation banning all activities in step 4 not related to fixed, ground-based ABM systems), it left open the possibility that it could choose to follow the broader interpretation at any time in the future.

By 1986, the Soviets had evidently come to recognize that their position was unlikely to help bring pressure on the United States to change its position. In May of that year, they tabled a proposal in Geneva calling for both sides to agree not to withdraw from the ABM treaty for a period of 15–20 years. Moreover, they seemed to define more modestly the scope of the treaty's strictures on research, development, and testing of space-based systems. Specifically, the Soviets seemed to propose that the superpowers agree that research within laboratories on technologies or subsystems relevant to space-based BMD is permissible, but that any field testing beyond labs was banned. That is, they would draw the line somewhere within step 2, depending on how loosely one defined the term "laboratory."

---

* The term "other physical principles" appears in the text of the ABM treaty. It refers to mechanisms for BMD that did not exist in 1972 (for example, lasers).

Since 1986, the Soviets have gradually shown yet more flexibility in their approach. By mid-1988 they seemed prepared to accept as the link between the START and ABM treaties a bilateral declaration of intent to observe the ABM treaty "as signed in 1972." They also wish to couple this declaration with a provision in the START treaty (either unilateral or bilateral) granting either party the right to suspend compliance with the START treaty in the event of a material breach of the ABM treaty by the other side.

Given the two sides' divergent views of the meaning of the ABM treaty, it is significant that the Soviets are no longer insisting on a declaration that commits both sides to observe the treaty "as signed *and ratified* in 1972"—language they tried (unsuccessfully) to have inserted into the final communiqué of the Washington summit in December 1987. We conclude that the Soviets are now prepared to acquiesce to the testing in space of *some* subcomponents of BMD systems (step 3 activities), in effect, opting for a unilateral interpretation of the treaty and relying on moderate and liberal elements in the United States to impose this interpretation on the administration. The Soviets still insist that neither side may test full components or integrated elements of a space-based BMD system and, of course, that no BMD system may be deployed other than the 100 fixed, ground-based interceptors permitted in the treaty. In short, the Soviet position seems to have returned to a balanced, traditional interpretation of the treaty— the view that prevailed among observers on both sides prior to President Reagan's Star Wars speech and all of the *Sturm und Drang* that has followed.

One cannot so neatly characterize an "official" American position with respect to either the ABM treaty or the purposes of the SDI program. Regarding the interpretation of the treaty, former Secretary of Defense Harold Brown has written that "the Soviets, the U.S. Congress, and the bulk of the non-governmental security community interpret the ABM treaty one way, the Reagan administration in another."[1] And while the administration continues to adhere formally to its broad interpretation, the date for the first U.S. test of an ABM component unambiguously in violation of the treaty's traditional interpretation keeps slipping further into the future.

It is even more difficult to determine with precision the purposes and objectives of the SDI program itself. The president's March 1983 speech held out the vision of a defense shield that could more or less comprehensively protect the U.S. population from an attack by strategic ballistic missiles.[2] The administration's *National Security Strategy of the United States,* published almost four years later (and following the expenditure of some $10 billion on SDI) presents a less-ambitious set of goals. It states that the SDI "offers an opportunity to shift deterrence to a safer and more stable basis through a greater reliance on strategic defenses." Such defenses, it adds, "could substantially enhance deterrence by injecting great uncertainties into Soviet" calculations. And it claims that "less than perfect defenses could significantly increase stability."

While the deployment of large-scale ballistic missile defenses by the United States would indeed increase the uncertainties confronting Soviet attack planners, one must assume that such deployments would be accompanied by Soviet defense deployments on a similar scale. Thus uncertainties regarding the effectiveness of U.S. strategic nuclear forces would also be increased. The net effect on deterrence of these two-sided deployments of defenses would be, at best, ambiguous. Moreover, we have already demonstrated why partially effective nationwide defenses would undermine both arms race and first-strike stability by raising the prospect of conditional survival. Consequently, the administration's statements regarding SDI's purposes have provided neither a clear description of the direction in which our policies are to take us nor a sound rationale for why we ought to go there.

Choices for the Next Administration

Despite (or perhaps because of) all of the visibility and resources accorded to the issue of ballistic missile defense in the Reagan administration, its successor will come to office with anything but a national consensus about the meaning of the ABM treaty and the future role of strategic defenses in American security. Decisions will be needed in this area in order to accomplish the following objectives:

- Complete the START treaty
- Structure a multibillion dollar BMD and air defense research program
- Set a broad and coherent course for future efforts to devise U.S. strategy, craft arms control proposals, and shape strategic force structure.

What should the next president do about all of this? The answers lie in an examination of the ways in which strategic defenses can contribute to U.S. security.

In approaching this subject, it is helpful to conceive of a series of basic types of strategic nuclear balances (what we call "worlds") that can exist between the superpowers, given varying levels and types of offensive and defensive weapons deployments on both sides. After describing these worlds in terms of their offense-defense relationships, one can draw general conclusions about the nature of three critical attributes in each—societal vulnerability (also called damage-limiting capability), arms race stability, and first-strike stability.

Table 1 illustrates in summary fashion six such worlds—in our view, the universe of distinctive possibilities—by placing them on a continuum of deployed defense potential. Associated with each world is an option for the deployment of strategic defenses.* Let us explore briefly the major attributes of each of these worlds. Note that in each case we assume that the Soviet Union essentially matches the level of U.S. BMD with like deployments of its own.

- *World 0—No additional deployments.*

This option accepts the existing level of strategic defense in the United States (and the Soviet Union). Mutual assured destruction prevails as both sides' populations and urban-industrial assets are vulnerable to attack. As shown in the figure, this world offers favorable conditions in terms of both first-strike and arms race stability. Neither is guaranteed or automatic, of course. Maintenance of first-strike stability requires that both sides modernize offensive forces as needed in light of evolving threats to those forces. Arms race stability depends on a measure of cooperation. But the incentives to add more and more offensive forces to one's arsenal in this world are quite small.

- *World 1—ABM treaty ceiling.*

Although deploying the number of interceptors permitted by the treaty is advocated by some in the United States, the world it would lead to is largely indistinguishable from world 0 in terms of vulnerability of urban-industrial regions, first-strike stability, and arms race stability. Various proponents of this option in the United States call for the reactivation of the U.S. ABM site at Grand Forks, North Dakota. Deploying 100 exoatmospheric and endoatmospheric ABM interceptors there would increase very marginally the price to attack U.S. ICBM fields and bomber bases in the area, but would not significantly affect first-strike stability.

Alternatively, the United States could choose, as the Soviets have done, to deploy its permitted ABM site around its capital. This would protect the national command authorities in the Washington, D.C.

---

* For simplicity, we focus here on the options for deploying ballistic missile defenses. Proportionate levels of air defense would be associated with each of these.

Table 1: *Options for Strategic Defenses*

	World					
	0 *No Additional Deployments*	*1* *ABM Treaty Ceiling*	*2* *ALPS*	*3* *Extensive Point Defenses*	*4* *Competitive Deployments*	*5* *Cooperative Transition*
Level of Deployed Defense Potential	Current (nil)	1 site; 100 interceptors	3 sites?; nationwide coverage	Multiple sites; ground-based	Very high; space-based and ground-based interceptors	Medium?; robust, nationwide defenses
Regime	<------------------Offense-dominant------------------>				Mixed	Defense-dominant
Damage Limiting Capability	<------------Mutual assured destruction *------------>				Conditional survival	Assured survival
First-Strike Stability	<------------Stable------------>			?	Unstable	Stable
Arms Race Stability	<------------Stable------------>			Unstable	Unstable	Stable

*World 2 offers population protection against very small ballistic missile attacks.

area from a small accidental or third-country ballistic missile attack. But a determined attack could easily overwhelm the system. Moreover, significant political hurdles, including cost, local opposition to the deployments, and nationwide opposition to expenditures for protecting only "the bureaucracy," have prevented serious consideration of this option.

In short, world 1 differs little from today's world; it just costs more to live there.

● *World 2—Accidental launch protection system (ALPS).*

Senator Sam Nunn has suggested that the United States examine the feasibility of deploying a very "thin" nationwide ballistic missile defense system that would be capable of intercepting a small number of RVs that might be directed against the United States in an unauthorized or accidental release of a ballistic missile or an attack by a small third country. Essentially, this option would provide the BMD equivalent of our current forces for continental air defense. These forces provide the capability to enforce sovereignty over our airspace in the face of very small air attacks. Pursuing an ALPS option would almost certainly necessitate a revision of the ABM treaty, since coast-to-coast coverage of either superpower's landmass with long-range, ground-based exoatmospheric interceptors could not be achieved from a single site.

Mutual assured destruction would continue to prevail in world 2, as each side's population would be protected across only a very small range of plausible scenarios.* This world would also retain the qualities of arms race and first-strike stability of worlds 0 and 1. Arms race stability might be jeopardized somewhat because once the infrastructure to support the thin nationwide defense system was installed, it would be easier to break out of a new ABM treaty regime to a world in which much more extensive defenses were deployed. Thus, mutual fears of such a breakout might be correspondingly exacerbated.

● *World 3—Extensive point defenses.*

World 3 features the deployment of a considerable level of defense potential, primarily in the form of ground-based interceptors. Deployments of these weapons are focused on the protection of key military installations, such as ICBM silo fields, command and control nodes, bomber bases, and logistic centers. The ostensible purpose of such deployments would be, in the words of the administration's statement

---

* As discussed below, it is not fully clear what types of realistic attacks an ALP system might be designed to cope with.

on national security strategy, to "enhance deterrence by injecting greater uncertainties into Soviet calculations." In particular, U.S. BMD under this option would be directed toward decreasing the reliance of silo-based ICBMs on a prompt launch under attack order for survivability.

Deployments of defenses under this option are arbitrarily kept at a level below that required for conditional survival, in order to distinguish world 3 from world 4. Thus, the urban-industrial infrastructure of both sides would remain vulnerable to both a first and a second strike. The net impact of BMD at this level on first-strike stability is ambiguous: If the deployment of these defenses could be strictly limited by mutual agreement to the protection of ICBM silos and bomber bases, the price of attacking these retaliatory assets would rise and stability would be increased. On the other hand, if the coverage afforded by these interceptors spilled over to other regions of each country, a retaliatory attack would have to cope with defenses in these regions and first-strike stability would be commensurately undermined.

Finally, as larger numbers of interceptors and battle management sensors, such as phased array radars, were deployed by both sides, arms race stability would become increasingly tenuous. Both sides would be tempted to deploy more defenses in order to reach at least unilateral conditional survival. Fearing that the adversary might achieve such a capability, each side would be tempted to proliferate offensive systems as well, perhaps in combination with BMD countermeasures designed to saturate, evade, confuse, and suppress the adversary's defenses.

- *World 4—Competitive deployments.*

The world likely to result from this option—conditional survival—would be unattractive in all dimensions. Here, at least one side (and possibly both) has deployed enough defense potential to survive a major nuclear exchange *if and only if it strikes first*. Thus, as noted earlier, the situation is first-strike unstable: Enormous incentives would exist, especially in a crisis, for one or both sides to launch a first strike. World 4 is also arms race unstable because each side will work feverishly to deprive the other of conditional survival. In a competitive situation, this can theoretically be done only by deploying more defenses, more offensive forces and countermeasures, defense suppression capabilities, or (the most likely course) all three in combination. Any such arms race at current levels of strategic forces would be ruinously expensive. Yet, despite this expenditure of resources, the security of both sides would be dramatically worsened in comparison with that of all other worlds.

• *World 5—Cooperative transition.*

Assured survival is a somewhat more modest goal than "perfect" population defense, or the leakproof "astrodome" defense sometimes associated with President Reagan's descriptions of his vision of the future. It seems virtually impossible that we will ever be able to prevent a determined adversary from being able to detonate weapons of mass destruction in at least a small number of our cities. Assured survival, then, means that following an attack, the vast majority of our population, along with the political and economic infrastructure needed to recover from the attack, would remain largely intact.

The weight of evidence available to date suggests strongly that assured survival cannot be achieved in the face of a large-scale, adaptive offense. Numerous studies of the problem have concluded that many countermeasures are available to a technologically advanced nation seeking ways to frustrate its opponent's BMD and air defense systems and that these countermeasures are likely to be far less expensive than the responses available to the defender.[3] At a minimum, attempting to achieve assured survival under such conditions would be fraught with the dangers of passing through (and getting mired in) world 4. To minimize this danger, a transition to assured survival would have to be a cooperative affair in which both the United States and the Soviet Union deployed defenses and simultaneously eliminated offensive forces according to a carefully devised and agreed-upon timetable.

World 5 would offer arms race stability because both sides would deploy defensive systems large enough to cope with any conceivable cheating in the deployment of offensive forces. Neither side would have any great incentive to launch a first strike, since the outcome would be highly unpredictable and the strike might have little or no militarily significant impact on the other side. Note, however, that the survivability of both sides' defensive forces against a direct attack would be crucial to the maintenance of stability and deterrence.

Is world 5 technically feasible? Probably, but *only if* both sides are willing to reduce their offensive forces to very low levels. Because of the cost and technical advantages accruing to the offense, neither side appears to have the option to move toward unconditional assured survival—world 5—unilaterally.

On the other hand, if both sides were willing to reduce their offensive forces to very low levels (ideally, all the way to zero), robust defenses, at least against ballistic missile attacks, could probably be provided by a system that included few if any space-based elements. Ironically, given all of the attention devoted to SDI and ballistic missile defense lately, it might be more difficult to provide comprehensive protection against air attacks than against ballistic missile attacks. If both sides were prepared to eliminate essentially all of their designated nuclear delivery vehicles (bombers, ICBMs, SLBMs, SLCMs, and so forth), very few ballistic missiles would be left to provide a basis for circumventing treaty restrictions. However, thousands of long-range civilian aircraft and military weapons, such as fighter-bombers and conventionally armed SLCMs, would remain, any of which might be quickly or covertly configured to deliver nuclear weapons.*

Nevertheless, the point remains that the major hurdles separating today's world from world 5 are more political than technical in nature: Are the nuclear powers prepared to give up all or virtually all of their nuclear weapons and delivery capabilities in exchange for mutual assured survival?

Evaluating the Options

Disaggregating the problem of defense deployments as we have done can assist in evaluating the choices available to the next president. One can assess the costs, risks, and benefits associated with each of the six worlds, choose which of the six is preferred, and then devise force development and arms control strategies to move toward that world. The following conclusions emerge:

1. World 4 should be avoided at all costs. World 4 is both first-strike and arms race unstable. Populations remain vulnerable to a first strike. And world 4 is horrendously expensive. No rational leader would deliberately choose world 4 as an outcome, yet it is quite possible the United States and the Soviet Union could stumble into such a world.

2. World 0 is superior to worlds 1 and 3. Each of these three offense-dominant worlds offers first-strike stability, and none would protect U.S. urban-industrial centers in the event of an attack. Worlds 0 and 1

---

* These and other complications associated with an attempt to ban nuclear weapons (or reduce them to near-zero) would drive nations working toward such an arms control regime to attempt to place controls on nuclear warheads themselves and the fissile material needed to produce them, also a complex proposition.

offer arms race stability, while world 3 could have serious arms race instabilities. Yet it would cost $10 billion or more to deploy 100 effective interceptors at a single site (world 1), and hundreds of billions to deploy the more extensive defenses envisaged in world 3.*

World 3 could conceivably improve first-strike stability if it were carefully and cooperatively implemented. But first-strike stability is certainly adequate today. And if it were not, BMD would have to be cheaper in comparison to other measures—such as the deployment of mobile ICBMs, or raising bomber or SSBN alert rates—to be an attractive answer.

World 3 fairly well describes one of the proposals for BMD deployments being considered most actively in the U.S. government today: the "first stage" deployment option recommended by the Defense Science Board in the late spring of 1988.

3. Thus, only worlds 0, 2, and 5 are worthy of serious consideration. These three worlds offer both first-strike and arms race stability. Worlds 2 and 5 offer, to widely varying degrees, protection of U.S. urban-industrial assets as well.

Choosing between worlds 0 and 2 is almost an exercise in actuarial accounting: How much are we willing to pay for the ALPS insurance policy? The answer, of course, depends on both the cost of the policy and its potential utility. The first is far easier to determine than the second. Currently available technologies can probably support at reasonable cost† a thin nationwide BMD system that could, with reasonable confidence, protect U.S. population and territory from an attack that included a few ballistic missile RVs (or, more precisely, objects in a ballistic trajectory). The problem is that it is difficult to conceive of a plausible scenario involving an attack of only a few objects. The most likely attack resulting from an unauthorized release would seem to be a full boatload of SLBMs or the ten or so ICBMs under the control of a single launch control center. Such an attack could involve anywhere from ten to 300 RVs and perhaps hundreds more decoys and other

---

* There are other disadvantages to world 3 not captured by our three criteria. For example, deployment by the Soviet Union of interceptors at a large number of military installations would undercut and perhaps invalidate selective attack options used by the United States to extend the deterrent effects of its strategic nuclear forces downward to theater-level conflict. And Soviet BMD capabilities in world 3 might also threaten the viability of the British and French strategic nuclear forces.

† Preliminary estimates of the cost to deploy an ALPS with coverage of the entire continental United States vary between $8 billion and $15 billion.[4]

objects. It is not clear that a BMD system can be devised that is at once capable of coping with an attack of this size, affordable, and clearly distinguishable from a rather thick nationwide defense shield.*

The United States and, it is claimed, the Soviet Union have both implemented extensive procedural and technical measures to minimize the possibility of an accidental or unauthorized arming and launch of a nuclear weapon. If the two are serious about further protecting each other against such launches, it would seem wise for them to investigate the feasibility of "command destruct" mechanisms for their SNDVs. Such devices would allow national leaders to order the destruction of missiles (and, presumably, bombers) that had been launched without authorization. The standard argument against such devices is that they might, in wartime, be fooled by enemy broadcasts into destroying legitimately launched weapons. But surely the mind of man can conceive of coding devices that would preclude the unauthorized triggering of these detonators during the few minutes or hours that they were in powered flight en route to targets.†

Choosing between worlds 0 and 2 (both offense-dominant and stable) on the one hand and world 5 (defense-dominant and stable) on the other involves a fundamental choice among competing values: Is robust deterrence or assured survival preferable? We have already stated our view that nuclear weapons today play a critical role in deterring Soviet aggression and intimidation in areas along the Eurasian periphery important to U.S. security. Before an American president sets a course for world 5, he will want to assure himself (and U.S. allies) both that such a world is technically feasible and that the United States can protect its own interests and those of its allies in a world devoid of effective nuclear threats against the Soviet homeland. In our view, the latter condition almost surely must await wide-ranging and

---

* In the future, as technologies needed to produce nuclear weapons and long-range ballistic missiles proliferate, ALPS might become attractive as a means of protection from attacks by countries other than the Soviet Union. The emergence of such a threat to the United States seems far enough off that near-term deployments do not appear warranted. Given the rapid proliferation of ballistic missile weapons to Iran, Iraq, and other Eurasian countries, however, the Soviet Union might soon abandon this sanguine view of the problem. Ironically, then, it may be Moscow rather than Washington that will one day take the initiative to propose a revision of the ABM treaty.

† One approach to hedge against the possibility that destruction codes would be compromised would be to use several different command destruct systems within each force component.

Table 2: Policy Recommendations

Policy Area	World				
	0	1	2	3	5
ABM Treaty	Reaffirm traditional interpretation	---------->	Seek revision to permit expanded but still limited deployments		Seek revision to permit time-phased deployment of survivable, effective, nationwide defenses, and transfer of ABM technology to allies
	Strengthen monitoring arrangements		Strengthen monitoring arrangements	---------->	
Research on Strategic Defenses	Focus research on technologies for potential long-term application to air and ballistic missile defense	Emphasize development of both exoatmospheric and endoatmospheric ground-based interceptors	Emphasize development of ground-based exoatmospheric interceptors with large "footprint"	Emphasize development of both endoatmospheric and exoatmospheric interceptors	Redirect most funds now devoted to strategic offense to research and development on the most promising technologies for battle management, surveillance, and intercept of ballistic missile and air-breathing weapons

82

Offensive Strategic Nuclear Forces	Modernize forces as needed to enhance survivability, effectiveness	------->	Seek negotiated, phased reductions to very low (near-zero) levels of forces
	Pursue arms control agreements to strengthen stability	------->	Retain preferentially the most survivable forces during reduction phase
			Seek reductions in third country forces

83

fundamental changes in the nature of Soviet forces for theater warfare and in East–West relations generally. Again, world 5 cannot exist without the full cooperation of the Soviet Union and, perhaps, other nuclear powers as well. Thus, the president cannot unilaterally choose and pursue this option.

A summary of policy prescriptions relative to each option is provided in Table 2. (Policies for world 4 are not provided.)

Note that the top panel of the figure shows that *in no case do we see continued unilateral adherence to the broad interpretation of the ABM treaty as an appropriate policy*. We believe that the Reagan administration's broad interpretation flies in the face of both the letter and the spirit of the treaty as written and ratified. More to the point, it is not in the interest of the United States to permit (let alone encourage) the continued unraveling of the ABM treaty regime. Regardless of which world one wishes to pursue, U.S.–Soviet cooperation in the area of BMD deployments will be essential if the two sides are to avoid dangerous instabilities. Thus, a unilateral effort by the United States to develop and deploy a wide-area ballistic missile defense system (the essence of the current situation) is a recipe for world 4 (that is to say, disaster).

Moreover, for all of their futuristic glamor, space-based ABM components—be they tracking sensors, battle management systems, or intercepting devices—have some serious and inherent drawbacks. Most important, it is very difficult to make such components survivable. They would trace predictable orbits through space. Shielding and other means of self-protection would add weight and, hence, cost to each component. And whole constellations of even heavily hardened satellites could be disabled by a single nuclear detonation in space. In a defense dominant world, the survivability of defenses against attack would be as important to first-strike stability as the survivability of offensive retaliatory forces is today.

These and a host of other technical difficulties notwithstanding, proponents of SDI remain fixated on the "leverage" that would accrue to the defender if he could intercept ballistic missiles in the first few minutes of their flight, before all of the missiles' RVs and decoys could deploy.* But in world 5 assured survival could be achieved without the need for highly leveraged defenses simply by reducing offensive forces to extremely low levels. And while a thin layer of boost- and postboost-phase interceptors might provide an adequate ALP system, the very short time available for engagement of the booster and warhead "bus"

---

* This approach is known as boost-phase and postboost-phase intercept.

(on the order of 5–7 minutes) would likely be insufficient to permit control of the system by national command authorities.

Finally, any space-based BMD weapons would have inherent applications as antisatellite weapons as well. The merits and risks associated with ASATs are addressed in chapter 5. It may suffice here to state that ASATs and ballistic missile defenses based in space could be highly destabilizing, providing great advantages to the side that shoots first.

For all of these reasons, then, the United States seems ill advised to expend substantial amounts of money to develop and deploy a system of ballistic missile defenses that includes a sizable share of space-based components. Rather, U.S. interests are best served by maintaining and strengthening the ABM treaty until such time as a policy course toward some other world is chosen. The United States can and should conduct a broad-based BMD research program within the treaty's framework, as traditionally construed. Such a program could be funded at a level considerably lower than current budgets for the SDI program, yet it would allow the United States to explore a wide range of approaches to BMD, and it would provide Moscow with additional incentives to comply with the ABM treaty.

If the next president or one of his successors should choose to pursue worlds 2, 3, or 5, the United States could begin negotiations with the Soviet Union to revise the treaty. In the meantime, by adhering to the broad interpretation of the treaty, the United States risks burning its bridges before it gets to them.

Approaches to the Geneva Negotiations

What are the implications of this analysis for the practical question of how the next administration should frame its approach to the negotiations in the defense and space forum of the Geneva talks?

We have already shown why we believe it is in the best interests of the United States for the next president to return to a policy of strict adherence to the narrow interpretation of the ABM treaty. In order to minimize further erosion of the ABM treaty regime, he would be well advised to state this policy clearly and at an early point in his tenure, noting that his decision was not influenced by the Soviets' linkage of the treaty's interpretation to the success of START. Rather, his decision should be based solely on a recognition of the treaty's essential role in assuring stability in any desirable offense-defense regime.

We expect that such a statement would meet Moscow's concerns about the course of the SDI program for the duration of the next administration. But the Soviets may want to formalize in some manner the U.S. "re-reinterpretation" of the ABM treaty in order to bind the *next* administration after 1992 or 1996. Once President Reagan's successor has promulgated his position on the treaty, he will have three options with respect to the Geneva negotiations:

1. He can insist that his own statement of U.S. government policy should satisfy Soviet concerns
2. He can subscribe to a general formulation of both sides' intentions regarding the treaty, such as that discussed at the Washington summit
3. He can pursue an explicit, written, bilateral statement clarifying what research, development, and testing activities are to be permitted and prohibited by the ABM treaty.

A president who is ready to state authoritatively that the United States will abide by the traditional interpretation of the ABM treaty should have no substantive objection to a statement committing this nation to observe the treaty "as signed and ratified in 1972." Options 1 and 2, in fact, would have the same effect on the policies of President Reagan's successor. The distinction between them is their impact on future presidents. It might be easier for a future president to repudiate an earlier, unilateral statement of policy (option 1) than a bilateral formulation incorporated into the START framework (option 2). This perceived distinction might lead Moscow to press the next administration for such a formulation.

On the other hand, the ABM treaty contains a provision allowing either signatory to withdraw from the treaty following six months' notification if its "supreme interests" are jeopardized. Thus, any added commitment conveyed by the formulation in option 2 may be more imagined than real. Despite this, option 2 could be a source of domestic political feuding. Recall our assessment, stated in the previous chapter, that opponents of START in the United States would like to be able to accuse the next president of selling out SDI to the Soviets as the price for agreement on START. If the next president accepts the very words that the Reagan administration rejected ("and ratified"), treaty opponents will gain a plausible debating point, even though the legal significance of such a formulation may be nil.

Option 1, then, would seem preferable to option 2 on domestic political grounds. If the Soviets press for a statement like that of option 2, the next administration will have to make a political judgment as to whether the costs of acquiescing, if any, justify resistance to such a demand.*

Option 3 must be judged against wholly different criteria—namely, to what degree is it in the U.S. interest to clarify remaining areas of ambiguity in the ABM treaty? Recall from our discussion of the evolution of U.S. and Soviet positions since 1983 that, even among those who adhere to the narrow interpretation of the treaty, there are disagreements about what activities in step 3 (flight tests of subcomponents), if any, the treaty prohibits. Undoubtedly, future ABM and, perhaps, ASAT development and testing programs on both sides will propose activities that fall within this gray area.

One "experiment" (actually a demonstration) recently proposed by SDIO, for instance, was to launch small, guided rockets from a satellite to intercept orbiting objects. While such a test clearly runs counter to the spirit of the ABM treaty, it might be argued to be technically in compliance with the treaty if the rockets' velocity were judged insufficient for an effective ABM system, if the satellite's engagement capacity were minimal, if the system could be plausibly described as an ASAT, or if other characteristics inherent to an operational weapon system were absent. Such arguments could be made in defense of a wide range of other tests as well—for example, tests of space-based lasers, mirrors in space for directing energy from ground-based lasers, or space-based rail guns.

Issues regarding the legality of such experiments can, of course, be referred to the Standing Consultative Commision (SCC) on a case-by-case basis.† But it may prove beneficial to both sides to seek a mutual understanding of the treaty's application in these areas before individual cases arise. On the other hand, reaching agreement on these issues might prove to be a tedious and time-consuming process. The next administration will want to avoid holding START hostage to the ABM treaty clarification process.

---

* Of course, General Secretary Gorbachev may have domestic political factions of his own to consider. Specifically, there may be elements within the Soviet leadership who will press for as strong a commitment as possible from Washington to abide by the narrow interpretation of the treaty. As a final twist, President Reagan's successor may be attracted to the idea of making it more difficult for future presidents to tamper with the interpretation of the ABM treaty.

† The SCC was established by Article 13 of the ABM treaty in order "to promote the objectives and implementation" of the treaty's provisions. Since its creation in 1972, the United States and the Soviet Union have used the SCC as a forum for the discussion and resolution of a number of questions regarding compliance with the ABM and SALT treaties.

On balance, then, it may prove wisest to pursue option 1, hoping to convince Moscow to accept an authoritative statement by the administration that the traditional interpretation of the ABM is the only correct one. Option 2—formally tying continued compliance with the START treaty to a continuation of the ABM treaty regime—might also be judged acceptable. Finally, it should be recognized that considerable ambiguity will remain concerning the ABM treaty's applicability to flight tests of sensor and weapon technologies that could serve as a basis for space-based, sea-based, air-based, or mobile land-based ABM systems but are less than full-fledged components of such systems. It would seem wise for the United States and the Soviet Union to address these ambiguities in a low-key manner, within either the existing SCC structure or perhaps in some ad hoc forum created by the defense and space portion of the Geneva talks.

4

Reducing and Disengaging Conventional Forces in Europe— The Vienna Talks

COMPLEX AS THEY ARE, negotiations over START and the ABM treaty appear simple and straightforward when compared with negotiations on conventional forces in Europe. While the former concern limited numbers of relatively comparable weapons, the latter encompass forces totaling millions of men and tens of thousands of pieces of equipment. Moreover, while START and the ABM treaty are discussed in small, bilateral negotiations, the new conventional force talks to be convened in Vienna will be conducted under the auspices of the Conference on Security and Cooperation in Europe (CSCE) in two separate multilateral sets of talks and will involve as many as thirty-five nations. Finally, while the operational strategies of the United States and the Soviet Union for employing nuclear weapons of intercontinental range appear to be broadly similar, NATO and the Warsaw Pact—the two antagonists at the center of the Vienna talks— have fundamentally different strategies for employing their theater-based forces.

Given these complicating factors, it would be foolish to expect rapid progress in the upcoming Vienna talks on either force reductions or new confidence- and security-building measures (CSBMs). Indeed, the political and military stakes and uncertainties surrounding the talks are so great that NATO has found it difficult even to formulate an agreed-upon negotiating position. Yet, it seems intuitively reasonable that after a standoff of more than forty years between East and West in Central Europe, it should be possible to take at least initial steps toward reducing and disengaging two of the most powerful peacetime military forces the world has ever known, without endangering the security of either side.

In this chapter we shall describe the scope and objectives of the two new sets of negotiations on forces in Europe, analyze the motivations of both the United States and the Soviet Union as they relate to these talks, assess the major contending approaches to these negotiations currently vying for acceptance in the West, and, finally, offer some broad policy prescriptions.

What Are the New Vienna Talks?

It is widely anticipated that some time in late 1988 or 1989, two sets of negotiations will get under way in Vienna. Both negotiations grew out of the latest review conference associated with the Helsinki accords that were concluded at the Conference on Security and Cooperation in Europe in the Finnish capital in 1975. One set—the Conventional Stability Talks (CST)—will involve the twenty-three nations of NATO and the Warsaw Pact. CST is concerned primarily with structural arms control, focusing on reductions in conventional forces deployed "on land from the Atlantic to the Urals."[1]

A second set of talks will involve thirty-five European nations, adding neutral and nonaligned states to the members of the two alliances. This forum, an offshoot of the Conference on Disarmament in Europe (CDE), will seek to develop new CSBMs for Europe. Operational arms control measures likely to be examined in these negotiations will include constraints on peacetime military activities; data exchanges and observation measures to increase each side's capability to monitor the other's military activities; and consultation, crisis avoidance, and crisis management measures designed to provide improved mutual understanding and a framework for sustaining communications and fostering cooperation in the event of serious political-military crises. This effort will seek to build upon the initial set of CSBMs agreed to at Stockholm in 1986. These measures included commitments by all signatories to do the following:

- Provide advance notification of all ground force exercises involving 13,000 or more troops or 300 or more tanks. Exercises involving 75,000 or more troops must be announced at least two years in advance; those involving 40,000–75,000 require one year's notice
- Invite all signatory countries to send observers to ground force exercises involving more than 17,000 troops. (Air and sea exercises are excluded.)

- Permit up to three short-notice inspections of forces each year to ensure compliance with the above provisions. (These inspections may be carried out on land or from the air by teams from countries not allied with the inspected nation; the inspected nation would provide the aircraft for airborne inspections.)[2]

The two sets of talks will replace the talks on mutual and balanced force reductions (MBFR), which have borne little tangible fruit since their inception in 1973.

The Purposes of Conventional Arms Control

The three perennial purposes of arms control we have applied to other realms apply to the realm of conventional forces as well: Limits on the overall size, structure, activities, and deployments of conventional ground and air forces are intended to strengthen first-strike (or, in this case, "conventional") stability, arms race stability, and political stability. The potential contributions of conventional arms control agreements—both structural and operational—to the second and third types of stability seem self-evident. And operational arms control measures that render more problematic mobilization, forward deployment, and surprise attack clearly can increase conventional stability by reducing the chances for a successful offensive by a would-be aggressor. However, designing structural arms control measures to increase conventional stability in Central Europe—the problem that lies at the heart of the CST negotiations—seems to be far more complicated.

Before delving into the issues associated with conventional arms control, it is worth examining the differing motivations brought to the negotiations by the United States and its allies on the one hand and by the Soviet Union and Warsaw Pact states on the other.

U.S. and NATO Objectives

At the broadest level, the United States and its allies would like to achieve at Vienna what they have been unable to attain in decades of unregulated East–West military competition: rough equality between the forces of NATO and the Warsaw Pact. NATO would also like to erect, via negotiation, additional impediments to a successful surprise or mobilized attack by Warsaw Pact forces.* Obviously, if these two

---

While the geographic scope of the Vienna talks—"from the Atlantic to the Urals"—encompasses all of Europe, including NATO's northern (Scandinavian) and southern (Mediterranean/Turkish) regions, the primary focus will likely be Central Europe, where the largest concentrations of NATO and Warsaw Pact military forces confront one another.

conditions could be achieved, NATO's security would be considerably enhanced. Yet, few observers believe that Moscow is prepared to reduce Warsaw Pact forces in the central region significantly without getting in return some substantial reductions from NATO.* And it has been difficult for NATO to identify what, if anything, it should be prepared to give up in return for the Warsaw Pact's eliminating or reducing its substantial numerical superiority in virtually every category of weapon counted.

As if this basic problem were not daunting enough, proponents of "nonprovocative defense" schemes (first in the West and now among some civilian defense specialists in Moscow) have complicated matters further by calling for the abandonment of traditional force structures in favor of forces equipped and deployed in radically different ways. They insist, with some justification, that reductions in conventional forces as presently configured in Central Europe will not increase stability unless they are accompanied by measures to restructure these forces in ways that would reduce their capabilities for offensive action.

While there seems to be some merit to these arguments, they tend to overlook the fact that, considerations of negotiability aside, simply reducing or eliminating the Warsaw Pact's numerical advantages in key categories of weapons would, in and of itself, substantially improve NATO's ability to defend itself. Those who advocate the radical restructuring of conventional forces tend also to classify particular types of equipment (typically, tanks, armored fighting vehicles, artillery, and interdiction aircraft) as being inherently offensive in nature. As we shall argue later in this chapter, such a classification can be dangerously misleading.

Of course, NATO governments bring other motives to the Vienna talks as well. One of the most important of these is to demonstrate to Western publics that NATO is at least as eager as Moscow to reduce East–West military competition through new arms control agreements. Under Mr. Gorbachev's leadership, the Soviet Union has been widely perceived as having seized and held the initiative in arms

---

* The central region referred to in this section is considerably larger than the central European area to which this term is generally applied. Specifically, we include the territory of the Benelux countries, Denmark, the Federal Republic of Germany, and France on NATO's side, and the Czechoslovakia, German Democratic Republic, Poland, and the three westernmost military districts (the Baltic, Belorussian, and Carpathian districts) in the Soviet Union on the side of the Pact. This encompasses all of the major areas from which forces would be drawn during a war in Central Europe; yet it is considerably smaller than the entire Atlantic-to-the-Urals region.

control. Whatever Moscow's actual intentions regarding the future course of the arms control process (the subject we shall turn to next), General Secretary Gorbachev and the men around him have convinced many in the West that they are prepared to consider sweeping changes in heretofore intractable military situations. Whether or not NATO is fully prepared to meet these Soviet initiatives with comprehensive proposals of its own, the Alliance cannot afford to ignore Mr. Gorbachev's pronouncements or to dismiss them as mere propaganda.

Another motivation, similar to the one that prompted NATO's proposal of the late 1960s and early 1970s to open the MBFR talks, is to forestall unilateral reductions in conventional forces by NATO nations in general and by the United States in particular. The need for bargaining chips in SALT and START has served successive American administrations well as an argument for the development of new nuclear weapon systems. Likewise, the Congress will be reluctant to cut U.S. forces in Europe as long as there remains a realistic possibility of getting Soviet and Warsaw Pact reductions in return. Put another way, if eventual unilateral reductions in U.S. or allied forces are, for economic or other reasons, more or less inevitable—a proposition that for some reason seems to be gaining increasing currency in the West—it makes eminently good sense to pursue negotiations aimed at getting something in return.

Soviet/Warsaw Pact Objectives

Do the Soviets, like NATO, fear being attacked in Central Europe? If they do, it is hard to see why, on the basis of an examination of the forces deployed there by both sides. As we shall see later in this chapter, the Warsaw Pact has achieved a substantial degree of numerical superiority in most measures of conventional weaponry in Central Europe. In sizing up the military balance, Soviet leaders no doubt take into consideration a number of nonquantifiable factors such as relative proficiency of personnel, the loyalty of non-Soviet Warsaw Pact forces, and qualitative asymmetries in individual weapons categories that could undermine their confidence in the potential effectiveness of their military machine in actual combat. But bilateral arms control measures cannot readily address these factors and, in fact, might make them more salient by undercutting Soviet numerical advantages. In fact, structural arms control in Central Europe can be portrayed as offering little more to the Soviet military than an invitation to give up hard-won advantages in deployed forces. What, then, might the Soviets hope to get out of the Vienna talks?

Part of the answer must lie in the Soviets' evident interest in furthering the process of denuclearization. Mr. Gorbachev's various proposals to eliminate nuclear weapons have been roundly criticized in the West as designed to make the world safe for Soviet conventional aggression. Because the West relies on nuclear weapons in part to help offset unfavorable balances in conventional forces in Eurasia, Moscow must at least *appear* willing to redress these imbalances if its proposals for large-scale nuclear reductions are to be taken seriously.

Additionally, Moscow appears to hope that the new round of talks will create opportunities to press NATO toward reductions in its nuclear capabilities. Most of NATO's member states will be very reluctant to consider proposals that would lead to further reductions in the Alliance's theater-based nuclear forces. Yet voices are heard across the political spectrum in West Germany calling for negotiation of a "third zero" agreement that would eliminate the shortest-range missiles and nuclear artillery shells from Central Europe.* Although the Soviets are pushing for new, separate talks on further reductions in theater nuclear forces, Moscow clearly intends to use the CST negotiations to gain reductions in NATO's primary long-range nuclear delivery systems, its dual-capable fighter-bomber aircraft.

Participation in revivified conventional arms control negotiations is also consistent with the evident Soviet desire to revive East–West détente. Mr. Gorbachev and company apparently seek a more cooperative and less-confrontational relationship with the West in part to gain expanded access to Western technology and credits and to contain the costs of the arms competition.

The central role of perestroika in Mr. Gorbachev's political program is well known. To the degree that the Soviet leader perceives the need to divert additional resources—financial, material, and human—to the tasks of economic modernization and innovation, he may find his country's very large, costly, and labor-intensive conventional forces an attractive target for cuts. This was the approach taken by Nikita Khrushchev in the late 1950s and early 1960s, when he tried to accelerate Soviet economic performance.

A detailed examination of the economic pressures facing the Soviet leaders and their possible impact on allocations of resources to defense is beyond the scope of this chapter. It should be noted, however, that Khrushchev and other Soviets have periodically complained of the

---

* The INF treaty has been dubbed the "double zero" agreement because it will eliminate long- and shorter-range INF missiles, defined as those having a maximum range of more than 1000 kilometers and 500–1000 kilometers, respectively.

priority accorded the "metal eaters" of the heavy and defense industries. Increasingly, proponents of large-scale conventional force modernization will also become "silicon eaters": demanding scarce, high-technology goods and expertise sorely needed throughout a stagnant economy.

Given the West's superior capacity to produce quality, high-technology weapons, General Secretary Gorbachev may seek an agreement limiting forces in Europe that somehow restricts qualitative improvements to Western forces. Soviet military writings in the 1980s have reflected serious concern about the potential ability of forces equipped with new, high-technology weapons to invalidate the Soviet military's strategy for (and investment in) offensive maneuver warfare based on the employment of massed armored formations. Indeed, the Soviet military has been working for years on developing operational and technical countermeasures to systems such as "reconnaissance-strike complexes" and other prospective elements of a NATO capability to attack follow-on forces that remain as yet in the design and development stages in the West.*

While it is difficult to conceive of an agreement that would directly limit or proscribe qualitative improvements in military capabilities, Mr. Gorbachev may be banking on the atmospheric effects of a series of arms control agreements and accommodating Soviet rhetoric to undercut Western force improvements indirectly through decreased willingness to support defense expenditures.

Demographic factors also provide a potential impetus for reductions in Soviet conventional forces, which account for the lion's share of the over 5 million personnel serving in the Soviet armed forces. The size of the eighteen-year-old male cohort of the Soviet population that becomes eligible each year for the semiannual call-up of conscripts has been declining steadily since 1979, when it reached its postwar high of nearly 3 million. It probably reached its nadir, at just over 2 million, in 1988, and will now rise slowly.[3]

The changing ethnic composition of the Soviet population is accentuating the effects of this population squeeze. Ethnic Russians constitute less than one-half of the draft-age male cohort today; Muslim-Turkic peoples account for approximately 25 percent, and they are expected to represent approximately 30 percent by the mid-1990s.[4] Many of these minority conscripts speak Russian poorly and are sus-

---

* The Soviets apply the term reconnaissance-strike complex (*razvedivatel'no-udarnyi kompleks*) to combinations of systems that provide near-real time surveillance of the battlefield and assessment of data, along with rapid attack capability.

pected of being unreliable in their commitment to the Russian-dominated Soviet state. Consequently, the Soviets have traditionally staffed their combat units with large majorities from the Slavic nationalities. These trends will make it difficult for the Soviets to maintain the preferred ethnic balance in their military units while also maintaining the current overall force structure.

All of these considerations beg the larger question of what Gorbachev might be trying to achieve through his foreign and security policies. Prior to the advent of new thinking in Moscow, it seemed possible to define rather clearly a set of Soviet objectives in Europe. The Soviets' disarmament and arms control proposals of the 1950s, 1960s, and 1970s suggest that they pursued three basic objectives:

- *Increase Soviet influence over the security affairs of all of Europe.*

The Soviets have long believed that their position as the dominant military power among European states entitles them to wield substantially greater influence over the external policies of all European states than is now the case.[5] This pursuit of a *droit de regard* over the affairs of Western Europe, with particular emphasis on defense activities, has led Moscow to try to reduce U.S. influence in Europe. Most importantly, the Soviets have consistently sought to contain, reduce, and eventually terminate the American military presence in Europe.

- *Contain the military power and political influence of Germany.*

Since 1945, the Soviet military occupation of East Germany has helped Moscow to ensure that Germany would not pose a serious threat to Soviet territory or to its sphere of influence in Eastern Europe. At several junctures in the postwar period, Moscow has sought further assurance in this regard by attempting to forestall the integration of the Federal Republic of Germany into the Western Alliance, and subsequently to limit West Germany's military capabilities. Moscow continues to seek to reduce West German military forces while also attempting to undermine Bonn's defense efforts by encouraging the growth of neutralist and pacifist elements within the Federal Republic.

Soviet preferences for a divided Germany and a neutral, weakened Federal Republic have sometimes conflicted with the goal of reducing the American presence in Europe. The Soviets for some time now have appeared to view West Germany's integration of the FRG into NATO as a factor helping to keep Bonn "under control." Continued American participation in NATO helps to discourage efforts toward a more vigorous, purely European defense cooperation, while it also reduces West German incentives to pursue a sovereign nuclear capability.

- *Contain within manageable limits the military power of the Western Alliance.*

To date, the Soviets have had to focus much of their diplomatic effort in Europe on the more immediate goal of constraining the military potential of NATO, accepting for the time being the presence of American forces in Europe and a Federal Republic of Germany firmly integrated into the Western Alliance. This effort is designed to fulfill the basic Soviet security objective of containing the military threat posed to Soviet interests in Europe by a strong, U.S.-led Western alliance. It also contributes to the maintenance and possible expansion of the margin of military advantage enjoyed by the East, a factor that has undoubtedly been thought to increase Soviet political leverage in both Eastern and Western Europe.

We cannot know whether and to what degree Mikhail Gorbachev and his immediate advisers still adhere to these basic objectives. The most optimistic interpretation of Soviet policies and statements under Mr. Gorbachev is that the new leadership has already largely abandoned these objectives, that it wants to redirect resources on a large scale toward economic modernization and restructuring, and that it is looking to arms control agreements with the West to provide a fig leaf of reciprocity in order to justify to conservative elements in Soviet political and military circles substantial reductions in their own forces. Alternatively, Mr. Gorbachev may simply be employing new, flexible tactics in pursuit of classic Soviet objectives.

The evidence available thus far is highly ambiguous. Moreover, even if the Soviet leader himself has adopted a fundamentally new approach to security, it is very much an open question whether he will succeed in replacing the traditional way of thinking, which sees international security as essentially a zero-sum game, with a new framework in which cooperation in the pursuit of mutually beneficial solutions to common problems dominates the agenda.

Western policymakers will therefore have to assume that Moscow's basic objectives with respect to conventional arms control remain at least selfish if not actually hostile, even as they try to capitalize on opportunities that may exist for improving stability in all three of its dimensions. Ultimately, the only way for Moscow to prove its sincerity regarding the application of Gorbachev's new thinking to international security matters is by making concrete concessions in conventional arms control negotiations.

Soviet Proposals

The Soviets took the initiative for new conventional force reduction negotiations in Europe in April 1986. At that time Mr. Gorbachev clearly signaled the Soviet intention to abandon any serious effort to reach agreement at the long-running but unproductive MBFR negotiations in Vienna.[6] Rather, Moscow was prepared to move on to a new, expanded set of talks directed toward the reduction of forces throughout Europe, that is, "from the Atlantic to the Urals."[7]

These new talks represent an expansion in the scope of MBFR, which encompassed only forces in Central Europe (East and West Germany, the Benelux countries, Poland, and Czechoslovakia), the "MBFR guidelines area." Accordingly, a broader range of nations will participate in the new talks. While this expansion in the scope of the conventional arms control negotiations increases their complexity, it also increases opportunities to explore agreements that can fundamentally affect the nature of the balance in Europe.

Old Thinking: The "Budapest Appeal"

At the conclusion of a meeting of the Warsaw Pact's Political Consultative Committee held in Hungary in June 1986, the Pact issued the so-called "Budapest Appeal," calling for a two-phase scheme of reduction in the new talks: an initial round of reductions in the late 1980s involving a cut of 100,000–150,000 troops from the forces of NATO and the Warsaw Pact; and a second round in the early 1990s, in which both NATO and the Warsaw Pact would reduce their armed forces and associated armaments by 25 percent, or some 500,000 personnel from each side.[8] This approach, featuring equal cuts by the two sides, is unattractive to NATO, given the Soviets' numerical superiority in the conventional balance in Europe.

Asymmetrical Reductions

Beginning in early 1987, General Secretary Gorbachev and other Soviet spokesmen began to sound a new theme, calling for the elimination of imbalances between NATO and Warsaw Pact forces. Specifically, Moscow has called for the elimination of imbalances in key weapons categories within the European theater via deeper reductions by the side that is ahead.[9] The Soviets claim that although each side enjoys advantages in certain weapons, a condition of overall military parity currently exists between NATO and the Warsaw Pact. Since early in 1987, Soviet spokesmen have said that the Pact is prepared to accept deeper cuts than NATO in tanks and possibly artillery, areas where they acknowledge that they possess substantial advantages. But they have also argued that NATO must be prepared to accept heavier reductions in what they claim are its more numerous ground attack aircraft and armed helicopters.

Throughout 1987 and the first half of 1988, the Soviets sought to include reductions in theater nuclear forces within the new European force reduction negotiations. By the summer of 1988 they had abandoned this effort and began pushing instead for the opening of new, separate negotiations on theater nuclear forces in Europe. These talks would seek the reduction and eventual elimination of nuclear-armed tactical ballistic missiles and other ground-based weapons with ranges less than 500 kilometers.

In the latter half of 1987 and in 1988, Soviet spokesmen became increasingly ambitious about the ultimate objective of conventional force reductions. Using the slogan of "reasonable sufficiency," Mr. Gorbachev and several others have called for the long-term restructuring of both NATO and Warsaw Pact forces in order to attain mutual postures of "nonoffensive" or "defensive" defense. Under such an arrangement, they assert, neither side would be capable of mounting a successful surprise attack or of carrying out large-scale offensive operations. This visionary goal runs directly counter to traditional Soviet military doctrine with its strong emphasis on the offensive. The continued ascendency of this doctrine is evinced by the introduction over the last decade of improved Soviet weapons, as well as numerous conceptual and organizational innovations with regard to the Soviet approach to war. These changes have been designed to improve the Warsaw Pact's ability to overwhelm NATO's defenses with a fast-moving, armor-heavy offensive campaign in Europe fought with conventional weapons.

A Multistage Proposal

In June 1988, Soviet spokesmen announced a new, long-term approach to the upcoming European force reduction negotiations. Lieutenant General Konstantin F. Mikhailov, a former general staff officer serving in the Disarmament Directorate of the Foreign Ministry, announced a new multistage proposal that blends elements of the new thinking and the older Budapest Appeal. The Soviets apparently will take this three-stage approach, which reportedly was presented to President Reagan at the Moscow summit in June 1988, at the opening round of the new talks in Vienna.

The first stage of the new Soviet approach involves three steps.[10] The first step would provide for an initial exchange of "official data" by NATO and the Warsaw Pact regarding the military forces on both sides throughout Europe. It would be followed by on-site inspections to verify the accuracy of the data. These two steps are designed to allow both sides to identify "imbalances and asymmetries" in the opposing forces. The third and final step of the opening stage, according to General Mikhailov, would be to implement reductions, presumably on both sides, in order to eliminate these asymmetries and thus bring the military capabilities of the opposing alliances into balance.

From the first stage onward, the Soviets also propose the creation of a north-south corridor through the center of Europe from which several selected armaments would be withdrawn. They would ban the storage of nuclear and chemical weapons within the corridor, which would extend 100 to 150 kilometers to the east and west of the inter-German and the West German-Czechoslovak borders. They propose also that both sides remove or substantially reduce "the more dangerous, destabilizing types of conventional arms"—presumably tanks, strike aviation, and possibly artillery and armed helicopters—stationed in this "zone of direct contact."[11] In their view, this zone would also be the target of both new confidence-building measures designed to limit strictly out-of-garrison troop movements and exercises, and of a demanding verification regime.

Having created this "thin out" zone and reduced key armaments to equal levels, NATO and the Warsaw Pact are to move on to the second stage. At that point, in accordance with the approach outlined in the Budapest Appeal, each side would reduce its armed forces by approximately half a million men, along with their associated equipment. Finally, this massive reduction would be followed by a third stage, in which the remaining armed forces on both sides would be fundamentally restructured so that neither would be capable of mounting offensive operations.[12]

CSBMs

The Soviets and their Warsaw Pact allies are also pushing several initiatives for "Stockholm II," the CSCE-sponsored, follow-on round of negotiations on confidence- and security-building measures in Europe slated to take place in parallel with the new force reduction talks. The most prominent of these initiatives calls for the creation of the "thin out" zone described above, which would reduce or eliminate certain weapons on each side of the line of contact between the two alliances in Central Europe. This proposal could be raised in the CST negotiations or in the talks on CSBMs.

Mr. Gorbachev and others have also been promoting a joint renunciation of the first use of nuclear weapons, the establishment of nuclear-free zones in northern Europe and the Balkans, constraints on naval and air activities in northern European waters and in the Mediterranean, limits on independent air and naval exercises throughout and around Europe, and a cap on the size of major air-ground exercises. The leaders of the Warsaw Pact have also called for the establishment of a NATO-Warsaw Pact "risk reduction" center to help diminish the dangers of war and assist in preventing surprise attack in Europe. Finally, the Soviets and their Pact allies have proposed a meeting of the supreme commanders of NATO and the Warsaw Pact and a gathering of military and political experts from the two opposing alliances for discussions of the current military doctrines of the two sides and the directions in which these doctrines are evolving.

Recent Soviet proposals for confidence-building measures have not been confined to Europe. Over the past few years General Secretary Gorbachev has suggested the convening of a conference on security in the Pacific region along the lines of the Helsinki conference held in Europe in the mid-1970s. He has proposed as well the creation of nuclear-free zones in the southern Pacific, the Korean peninsula, Southeast Asia, and the Indian Ocean, as well as reductions in naval activities in both the Indian Ocean and the Pacific, including limitations on the patrol areas of nuclear-armed ships so their weapons could not reach the territory of other signatory states. Finally, the Soviet leader has called for the negotiation of CSBMs for Asia that would provide for advance notification of ground, naval, amphibious, and air force exercises, and would place limitations on the size and frequency of naval exercises.[13]

NATO Proposals

Thus far, NATO governments have responded to this welter of proposals only in a general manner. At the NATO summit in March of 1988, the allies agreed on their primary objective in the Vienna talks. It is an ambitious one: "to establish a situation in Europe in which force postures as well as the numbers and deployments of weapon systems no longer make surprise attack and large-scale offensive action a feasible option."[14] NATO leaders also outlined the general approach they would take in the negotiations, noting that any agreement at Vienna should, among other things, do the following:

- Eliminate disparities in force levels through asymmetrical reductions by the East, including the elimination of tens of thousands of tanks and artillery pieces

- Encompass measures for "limitations and redeployments," as well as reductions in the pursuit of equal ceilings on specific categories of weapons
- Include "measures to produce greater openness of military activities, and to support a rigorous monitoring and verification regime"
- Include in this regime "the exchange of detailed data about forces and deployments, and the right to sufficient on-site inspections to be confident of compliance."[15]

By late 1988, after more than two years of consultations, the NATO governments had reportedly agreed upon most of the basic elements of the opening proposal they intended to table at the Conventional Stability Talks. The proposal will most likely specify the types of weapons they wish to see reduced, the ceilings they prefer for each category, and a schedule according to which reductions should take place.

The Conventional Balance

Part of the reason for NATO's tentativeness in approaching the subject of reductions has lain in uncertainties about the nature of the conventional balance in Central Europe: How one assesses the nature of the balance in the central region will largely determine one's views on what would constitute an acceptable CST outcome.

As noted above, the Soviet Union maintains that the military capabilities of the two alliances are essentially equal. There is a broad consensus among Western observers and officials, however, that NATO's conventional forces would be hard-pressed to cope with a Warsaw Pact offensive. General John Galvin, supreme commander of allied forces in Europe, for example, has stated that, in his view, should Warsaw Pact forces attack in Central Europe, he would be forced within 10–14 days to request authorization to use nuclear weapons in order to avoid defeat.[16] His immediate predecessor, General Bernard Rogers, shares that view. He also believes that the balance is deteriorating from NATO's perspective. He stated in 1987 that "if we're not going to let this gap [between NATO and the Warsaw Pact] continue to widen— and it does widen every year—every nation [in NATO] is going to have to do more."[17] The late General Maxwell Taylor, chairman of the Joint Chiefs of Staff under President Kennedy, agreed, stating that NATO's problem was endemic. In 1982, he wrote that since the French withdrawal from NATO's military command in the mid-1960s, "NATO has no communications zone of adequate depth behind its combat troops, and the U.S. forces have had to depend on supply lines . . . running dangerously close to the battlefront. . . . In the aggregate, these adverse logistical factors justify a conviction . . . that a sustained conventional defense is not possible."[18]

These professional soldiers undoubtedly based their views on their personal judgment of the likely outcome of war, given their understanding of the relative capabilities of both sides' forces, their strategies, and the conditions under which they would fight. In recent years, a number of organizations have devised computer-based models of these factors in order to help formulate more structured assessments of the probable course and outcome of combat in Central Europe under a wide range of conditions. The RAND Corporation has developed one such model, whose simulations broadly confirm the judgment of generals Galvin and Rogers. Typical results of such simulations show NATO losing 100 or more kilometers of territory (measured westward from the inter-German border) in thirty days of warfare following a Warsaw Pact invasion.[19]

A vocal minority of analysts are far more optimistic regarding NATO's prospects for a successful conventional defense. They typically argue that NATO could exploit its supposedly superior intelligence collection and command and control capabilities, its higher-technology weapon systems, its favorable terrain, and the inherent advantages that accrue to the side conducting a prepared defense, to hold the line against the Warsaw Pact's larger but less-flexible forces. Joshua Epstein, of the Brookings Institution, for instance, has developed a computer model that leads him to the conclusion that NATO today "has the material wherewithal to stalemate the Warsaw Pact," at least in cases involving relatively lengthy mobilization periods.*

Some portion of these gross disparities in analysts' estimates of the conventional balance may result from the natural conservatism of the military commander in assessing the adequacy of his forces. Frequently, commanders will be all too well aware of the "hidden" shortcomings and problems associated with their own forces, such as equipment unreliability, fragility of command and control networks, low supply levels, and inadequate training of troops. At the same time, they will be unaware of similar shortcomings in their adversary's forces or prepared to discount their significance.

A more important factor accounting for these disparities, however, is the enormously complex nature of modern warfare. Many quantifiable factors such as numbers of troops, weapons, and munitions; estimated weapons effectiveness factors; sortie and fire rates; and even weather can be loaded into a model, be it an explicit model inside a computer or

---

* Epstein's simulations, run over 91–136 days of combat, show NATO losing 0–7.1 kilometers of territory to a Warsaw Pact invasion.[20]

an implicit, judgment-based model in one's head. However, an equally large number of nonquantifiable variables such as morale, competence, leadership, and initiative are at work as well during a battle and a war. The ways in which all of these factors, tangible as well as intangible, interact are often poorly understood, unpredictable, and not amenable to mathematical expression.

Given the enormous uncertainty surrounding any assessments of the relative combat capabilities of NATO and the Warsaw Pact, how shall policymakers approach the job of formulating arms control proposals and force development plans? Can NATO accept some cuts in return for larger reductions in Warsaw Pact forces? At what rate of exchange? What capabilities are most important to NATO's conventional defense posture, and what additional capabilities are most needed? Models of warfare can provide valuable insights on some aspects of these questions. But they cannot and may never be able to provide a definitive characterization of the military balance at the theater level. Thus, other, more straightforward approaches are needed as well to inform our thinking. These include examinations of static measures of the balance and of the operational strategies of NATO and the Warsaw Pact.

Static Measures of the Balance

It is fashionable among defense analysts these days to deride "bean counts"—comparisons of total weapons or combat units deployed by two opposing forces—as inadequate measures of relative combat power. (The cognoscenti among defense analysts refer to such accountings as static measures of the balance. The use of an explicit model to simulate warfare yields dynamic measures.) Obviously, bean counts alone are inadequate, given the important role played by many of the intangible factors mentioned above in determining the outcome of battles. But bean counts are not irrelevant and they are relatively unambiguous: Both absolute and relative numbers of combat units and weapons available to opposing forces are major determinants of the outcome of warfare.*

Perhaps equally important, static measures play an important role in the development of perceptions of the political-military balance. The purpose of military forces is not to fight wars, except in extremis. Nations deploy military forces above all to deter attack, and secondarily to help ensure that they cannot be coerced by the threat of attack by an

---

* Force ratios, of course, are not always decisive determinants of the outcome of battles or wars. History is replete with cases in which numerically inferior forces have emerged victorious.

adversary. Military forces can also be used to underwrite implicit or explicit coercive threats aimed at altering the behavior of other states. The Soviet leadership, for example, might well believe that deploying conventional forces with a sizable degree of numerical superiority over the forces of its neighbors can provide a basis for extending its influence through the use—subtle or otherwise—of coercive threats. Precisely because dynamic assessments of the military balance are so complex and so rife with uncertainties, a clear-cut degree of Western inferiority in static measures can undermine Western willingness to resist Soviet coercion *regardless of the actual relative combat capabilities of NATO and Warsaw Pact forces.**

For all of these reasons, the numerical balance of forces matters. This balance is unfavorable to NATO more or less across-the-board. Figures 12 and 13 show the levels of some selected elements of NATO and Warsaw Pact forces. As Figure 12 shows, when forces available for combat in Central Europe are compared, Warsaw Pact divisions out-number NATO's in the central region by a margin of approximately 3:1 in peacetime. Under mobilized conditions, when both sides would have several weeks to bring reserve units up to full strength and to deploy forces to forward positions, the divisional balance improves, from NATO's standpoint, to 1.8:1.†

Individual Warsaw Pact divisions are generally smaller than those of NATO nations. A typical American or German division, for instance, comprises approximately 16,000 troops, whereas a Soviet division comprises 11,000–12,000. Despite this difference, the firepower associ-

---

* We say that numerical inferiority *can* undermine Western resolve because it seems for the most part not to have had such an effect to date. This can be accounted for largely by the existence of a sizable arsenal of nuclear weapons, in both Western Europe and the United States. As long as the prospects for large-scale nuclear use in response to a Warsaw Pact attack are not wholly incredible (a perception grounded in part on the state of the conventional balance), Moscow will find it difficult to actualize, vis-à-vis NATO, the coercive potential of its numerically superior conventional forces.

† Forces included in these counts are, for NATO, those of Belgium, Denmark, Luxembourg, the Netherlands, and West Germany, as well as those actually deployed in Central Europe from Britain, Canada, France, and the United States. For the Warsaw Pact, forces of Czechoslovakia, East Germany, and Poland are counted, as well as Soviet forces deployed in those countries and forces in the Baltic, Belorussian, and Carpathian military districts of the western Soviet Union. Many of these latter units of the Soviet Union's western military districts would be brought forward into East Germany and western Czechoslovakia during a mobilization.

ated with Pact divisions tends to be comparable or, in some cases, superior to that of NATO's larger divisions. This is because NATO divisions allocate more manpower to logistical support activities, such as supply and maintenance, than Warsaw Pact divisions. Thus, military manpower in Central Europe is somewhat more balanced than combat units and firepower.

In the MBFR, in fact, the Warsaw Pact negotiators insisted that the military manpower of the two alliances was essentially equal.

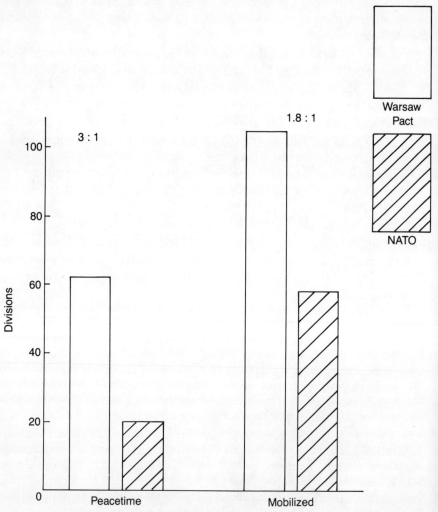

Source: The International Institute of Strategic Studies, *The Military Balance, 1986–1987*, London, 1987, pp. 42, 77, and 226.

FIG. 12. *Warsaw Pact and NATO Forces (and Ratios) in the Central Region*

They claimed that the Pact deployed 987,300 men under arms in the MBFR guidelines area, while NATO deployed 984,000.* NATO's figures were 1,125,000 for the Pact; 970,000 for NATO. (These numbers work out to a ratio of 1.16:1 in favor of the Pact.)

As Figure 13 shows, larger asymmetries appear to exist in the levels of weapons deployed by the two sides. When units available in a mobilized scenario are counted, equipment ratios range, by one count, from a Warsaw Pact superiority of 1.75:1 in ground attack aircraft and 3:1 in main battle tanks to 6:1 in surface-to-air missile (SAM) launchers deployed with ground forces.

Comparing the size of Warsaw Pact and NATO forces ("counting the beans") is not as straightforward a task as one might expect. Tallies of Warsaw Pact equipment (at least those available in the public domain) are not based on an actual census of the equipment. Rather, they represent, in most cases, an estimate derived by multiplying the number of Pact divisions known to be deployed by the number of items of each type of equipment normally deployed with such divisions. Thus, weapons and equipment in centrally held reserve stocks or deployed with nondivisional entities are often not included in these figures. Data for NATO's forces, by contrast, generally include all items of equipment available.

Of course, disparities in the quality and capabilities of individual items of equipment (sustainable rates of fire for artillery pieces, mobility and survivability of armored vehicles, range and accuracy of missiles, and so forth) can have significant effects on the balance. It is beyond the scope of this book to assess the net effect of such qualitative differences on the NATO–Warsaw Pact balance. However, the conventional wisdom among Western observers today is that the "qualitative edge" NATO forces were said to enjoy in the 1960s and early 1970s is being lost, at least in some areas.

Further difficulties arise in trying to aggregate weapons into categories for comparison. Many types of weapons defy easy categorization. For example, in counting and reducing forces it seems reasonable to differentiate fighter-interceptors, which are used to shoot down enemy aircraft, from fighter-bombers and bombers, which are optimized for ground attack. Yet both sides deploy aircraft—such as NATO's F-4 and F-16 and certain models of the Soviet MiG-21—with inherent capabilities for both missions. How are these multimission aircraft to be compared? Likewise, Soviet Mi-8 Hip helicopters are used primarily for

---

* As was mentioned earlier, the MBFR guidelines area encompassed the territories of Central European nations participating in the MBFR talks: the Benelux countries, Czechoslovakia, the two Germanies, and Poland.

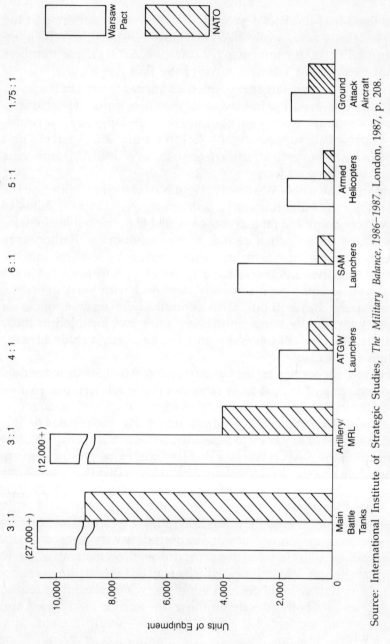

FIG. 13. *Comparative Deployments of Warsaw Pact and NATO Equipment in the Central Region*

Source: International Institute of Strategic Studies, *The Military Balance, 1986–1987,* London, 1987, p. 208.

108

transporting assault troops. But they have also been armed with missiles and rockets for ground attack. Should they be considered as "attack helicopters" even though they are generally used in roles different from those assigned to smaller, antitank helicopters, such as NATO's Cobra and Apache and the Soviet-built Mi-24 Hind?

There are many other examples of such ambiguous cases. Thus, even if the two sides can quickly agree on an overall count of weapons and equipment deployed by both sides, it seems certain that an important (and time-consuming) element in the Vienna talks will be the determination of which weapons to put into which categories. In some areas, such a categorization will be crucial to determining both the existing static balance of forces and the scale of reductions necessary to achieve compliance with any negotiated ceilings.

Such factors help to account for the wide variance in estimates of NATO and Warsaw Pact forces. One prominent analyst of European security issues, for example, has published figures showing ratios of Warsaw Pact to NATO forces in the MBFR guidelines area in Central Europe, such as 2.4:1 in main battle tanks, 4:1 in artillery, 1.5:1 in attack helicopters, and 1.9:1 in bombers and fighter-bombers. Most of these ratios are decidedly higher than those cited for the same region by the International Institute for Strategic Studies in London.[21]

Nevertheless, the overall picture is clear: Warsaw Pact forces enjoy substantial numerical superiority over NATO in most categories of weapons deployed in the central region and its immediate rear areas. And careful definitions of weapon categories and consistent counting practices will be required to establish an accurate, agreed-upon data base. Redressing these asymmetries should be one of NATO's major objectives in the Conventional Stability Talks. But the Alliance must be extremely careful in choosing what it might give up in exchange for reductions in Pact forces. It is necessary to examine the operational strategies of the two alliances in order to understand why this is so.

Operational Strategies

"Operational strategy" describes the ways in which theater-level military commanders plan to employ the forces available to them in the pursuit of their objectives. Recent Soviet claims to the contrary notwithstanding, the Warsaw Pact's operational strategy is quintessentially offensive in nature. Soviet military writings make it clear that in wartime, Warsaw Pact commanders would conduct a blitzkrieg-style offensive that would allow them to determine the time and place of major thrusts. Thus, the Pact could concentrate its forces at narrow sectors of the front to make breakthrough assaults. NATO, meanwhile, is forced for political and geographic reasons into a forward, relatively static defensive strategy. Because NATO cannot plan to cede large portions of the Federal Republic of Germany to Pact forces during an early phase of a war, allied forces must man a "thin blue line" stretched across the front from the Baltic to Austria.*

Tanks, armored fighting vehicles, artillery, and attack helicopters play a central role in the Pact's plans for offensive operations. Armored forces, operating in concert with massive fire support, are to pierce NATO's forward defenses in order to permit the attacker to insert exploitation forces of division size or larger through the resulting gaps. The purpose of these exploitation forces—operational maneuver groups and other second-echelon formations—is to cripple NATO's capability to respond to breakthroughs by interfering with Western reinforcement activities and command and control functions. In so doing, they would pave the way for larger forces to come into NATO's rear, encircling the West's forward corps, neutralizing remaining operational reserves, and seizing theater objectives at or beyond the Rhine.

For these reasons, many in the West have favored deep reductions in NATO and Warsaw Pact armored vehicles, artillery, and attack helicopters as a means of hobbling Soviet offensive capabilities. But the same types of weapons play a key role in NATO's operational strategy for defending its territory. Because NATO must spread its initial echelon of defending forces more or less evenly across the entire front, the only way it can cope with breakthroughs is to have operational reserve forces available with adequate firepower and mobility to engage and defeat exploitation forces soon after they breach NATO's forward defenses. The mobility, survivability, and firepower offered by armored vehicles, self-propelled artillery, antitank helicopters, and fixed-wing aircraft used in close air support make them ideal weapons for these operational reserve forces.

Likewise, aircraft used for ground attacks in rear areas can contribute to the Warsaw Pact offensive by damaging NATO's air bases, reserve forces, command and control posts, storage depots, airports and seaports of debarkation, and other rear-area assets. Yet NATO also relies heavily on such aircraft to attack Pact follow-on forces, supplies, and the roads and rail lines over which they move in order to prevent them from being brought forward in a timely, organized fashion and to reduce their strength before they reach the battle area. Enemy initial assault forces and exploitation elements can be attacked in this way,

---

* NATO plans to erect additional forward defense positions should the Soviets attack in northern Norway, northern Italy (through Yugoslavia or Austria), or Turkish and Greek Thrace.

disrupting the Pact ground force commander's scheme of maneuver. In summary, the very types of weapons that pose the greatest threat to NATO are precisely those most needed to defend against the threat.

In wartime, breakthrough assaults would likely occur simultaneously at several points along NATO's forward defense line. So many of NATO's forces are needed to cover the lengthy forward line that Allied commanders find it difficult to constitute operational reserve forces adequate to cope with breakthroughs that might occur. Thus, substantial reductions in NATO's forces could undermine NATO's operational strategy for coping with a Warsaw Pact invasion.

Pact forces, on the other hand, which are already considerably larger than NATO's, can concentrate in areas of their choice, while manning other sectors of the front more thinly. Because terrain limitations allow only a limited number of forces to be deployed opposite NATO's line in support of a breakthrough assault, the Pact commander would "stack up" his divisions in successive echelons in his rear area. Thus, while small reductions could cripple NATO's defense capability, even sizable reductions in Pact forces might not significantly diminish the combat power the Pact is able to direct against NATO in the opening days and weeks of a war.

Several implications emerge from this brief analysis of numbers and strategies. First, singling out specific types of weapons and equipment for reductions on the basis of their supposedly inherently offensive nature can be risky, because it could weaken NATO's defensive capabilities as much as or even more than it reduces the Pact's offensive punch.

Second, if NATO forces are to be reduced at all by a CST agreement, such reductions ought to be accompanied by much larger reductions in Pact forces, such that the Pact's combat power available to mount and exploit multiple breakthrough assaults in the opening days of a war would be significantly diminished.

Finally, NATO's most serious problems would appear to arise in so-called short-warning scenarios, in which neither side has time to mobilize fully prior to a Warsaw Pact attack. (Recall that the ratio of Pact to NATO divisions is 3:1 in peacetime versus 1.8:1 following a full mobilization carried out over thirty days or more.) Thus, measures to reduce the likelihood of a covert mobilization and surprise attack can make an important contribution to NATO's security.

It is important to keep these points in mind as we evaluate the alternative approaches to conventional arms control available to the next administration.

Options for Conventional Arms Control

Four basic, complementary approaches exist with the potential for increasing stability via conventional arms control. Forces can be reduced in number, restructured to diminish their striking power relative to defensive capabilities, and redeployed to make the mounting of offensive operations more difficult and time-consuming. In addition, rules governing the activities of forces in peacetime can be established to increase confidence that the adversary is complying with the arms control regime and to make more difficult and readily apparent the forward movement of forces required to support a major attack. The first two approaches—reductions and restructuring—will be the subject of the Conventional Stability Talks. Questions of more limited redeployments of forces, constraints on peacetime activities, and provisions to facilitate the observation of military activities will be the subject of the Stockholm II CSBM negotiations.

Using these basic approaches as an outline, let us briefly review a range of options.

Reductions

In framing a conventional force reductions regime, one must specify *what* is to be reduced, *how* reductions are to be implemented, and *how much* to reduce forces from existing levels.

What to Reduce? There seems now to be a consensus in both East and West that individual weapons and items of equipment represent the most useful metric for denominating a conventional arms reduction agreement. Ceilings on active duty military manpower alone—the basic approach taken in the abortive MBFR negotiations—are commonly rejected as being too difficult to verify and too easily circumvented. Put simply, it is far easier to conceal or to return to the theater a division's worth of personnel than a division's worth of equipment.

Having settled on hardware as the basis for denominating reductions, one must next determine what types of hardware to reduce and what types to leave unconstrained. The conventional wisdom has it that reductions should be focused on those weapons that can play the most important roles in the conduct of offensive operations. Tanks, armored fighting vehicles, artillery, ground attack aircraft, attack helicopters, and surface-to-surface missiles are the most commonly cited candidates for reductions according to this criterion.* By implication,

---

* Other items important to Warsaw Pact offensive operations but less often mentioned as candidates for reductions are tactical bridging equipment and vehicles for clearing mines and other obstacles.

other weapons, including fighter-interceptors, surface-to-air missiles, and infantry weapons, would be left unconstrained, as would certain support systems, such as reconnaissance platforms, radars, and electronic jamming devices.

Earlier in this chapter, we explained that a simple bifurcation of weapons into "offensive" and "defensive" categories is potentially dangerous, since NATO relies on both types to support its defensive operational strategy. In light of this, it seems better to think of all of the weapon types mentioned above as contributing to both sides' combat capabilities, whether applied to offensive or defensive operations. Thus, NATO must be wary of giving up too much in return for too little, a subject we shall turn to in a moment.

In our view, conventional force reductions should be focused on forces that best lend themselves to seizing and holding ground. This strategy points to cuts in main battle tanks, the linchpin of modern mobile maneuver warfare; artillery, their most crucial supporting element; and armored fighting vehicles, which carry the infantry into battle. These are the weapons deployed in the greatest numbers by both sides in the central region. NATO's primary negotiating objective should be to eliminate or sharply reduce Warsaw Pact superiority in these weapons, while retaining a sufficient number of them to support its own operational strategy.[22]

By any accounting, Pact numerical advantages in these areas are sizable. Are there other types of weapons that NATO might be able to agree to reduce bilaterally with the Pact as a way of making highly asymmetrical cuts in armor and artillery more palatable to Moscow?

We have already noted that the Soviets have placed NATO ground attack aircraft high on their agenda for cuts. They have apparently arranged their accounting scheme for these weapons in such a way as to show a higher total for NATO than for the Pact, and they have repeatedly asserted that NATO will be required to take deeper cuts to eliminate this imbalance. Most Western accountings, however, show an approximate balance or a slight Pact edge when truly comparable aircraft are counted. Thus, it is not clear that including ground attack aircraft in the talks would, in fact, be favorable to Moscow, at least on the basis of numbers alone. Nevertheless, Soviet military writers have long credited NATO's tactical aviation with making a potentially decisive contribution to the West's defensive capabilities. Therefore, even if NATO can demonstrate that the Warsaw Pact enjoys numerical superiority in this area, the Soviets may be happy to accept marginally greater cuts in their own tactical aviation in order to get reductions in what they perceive to be NATO's higher-quality ground attack capabilities.

Reductions in ground attack aviation, if implemented effectively, would reduce not only NATO's conventional defense capabilities but also its theater nuclear potential. As the Pershing and ground-launched cruise missiles are withdrawn from Europe in the wake of the INF treaty, land-based "dual-capable" tactical aircraft (those that can deliver both conventional and nuclear weapons) will shoulder an increasing share of the Alliance's long-range, theater-based nuclear delivery capability. Given simply the widespread concerns that the INF treaty is already seriously weakening NATO's theater nuclear forces, NATO policymakers will be loath to give up tactical aviation assets.

Moreover, ground attack aircraft—F-111s, Tornados, F-16s, A-10s, and others—also play a crucial role in NATO's conventional defense plans. They provide highly flexible capabilities for attacking Warsaw Pact forces in enemy rear areas, near the line of contact, and, should breakthroughs in the forward defense line occur, in NATO's rear area.

So real reductions in NATO's tactical aviation capabilities might be risky. But redeploying some aircraft to bases outside of the Atlantic-to-the-Urals region need not result in a serious diminution of NATO's wartime ground attack capabilities. Aircraft and aircrews withdrawn to the United States but retained in active service, for instance, could be returned to Europe in a day or two if the basing and support infrastructure necessary for operating the aircraft were maintained in the theater. The Warsaw Pact might resist such an approach as yielding only token reductions, but short of imposing global limits on the two alliances' tactical aviation (something the Soviets tried and failed to do through the INF talks), it is unclear how they might get more militarily significant reductions.

Another area where the Soviets are sure to press for reductions is in tactical and battlefield nuclear weapons. These include surface-to-surface missiles with ranges of less than 500 kilometers, nuclear artillery rounds, and atomic demolition mines (ADMs). Many of the consequences of reductions in these weapons are similar to those identified above for tactical aviation.

As Table 3 shows, the Warsaw Pact appears to enjoy numerical superiority in these weapons, especially in tactical, or short-range, ballistic missiles (TBMs). But recognizing that nuclear weapons play a more important role in NATO's deterrent posture than in the Warsaw Pact's strategy, the Soviets appear ready to reduce substantially or even eliminate these weapons through bilateral agreement.

These weapons provide the first rungs on NATO's ladder of nuclear escalatory options. As such, they play an important role in maintaining the credibility of NATO's deterrent strategy by providing a tangible

Table 3:   *Nato and Warsaw Pact Tactical Nuclear Forces in Central Europe*

Type of Weapon	Warsaw Pact	NATO†
Short-range ballistic missile launchers	560 SS-21/FROG 140 Scud	163 Lance 44 Pluton
TOTAL	700	207
Nuclear-capable artillery	3900	875 M-110 2160 M-109
TOTAL	3900	3035

Source: International Institute for Strategic Studies, *The Military Balance, 1986–87,* London, 1987, p. 208.
†Plus France.

connection between NATO's longer-range nuclear weapons and the course of the tactical land battle: A commander of a division faced with the prospect of being overrun by enemy forces might very plausibly consider resorting to battlefield nuclear weapons. Because these weapons present the Soviet military planner with the realistic possibility of escalation to nuclear use in response to a Warsaw Pact invasion, NATO leaders are reluctant to consider reductions in such weapons.*

As with tactical aviation, limits on nuclear-capable TBMs might also impinge upon NATO's conventional defense capabilities. The United States is currently developing two new ground-launched missiles with ranges of less than 500 kilometers: the Army Tactical Missile System (ATACMS, a ballistic missile) and the Joint Tactical Missile System (JTACMS, a cruise missile). Both are to carry specialized conventional submunitions designed for attacks on armored vehicles and other targets. In the INF agreement, conventionally armed missiles of range greater than 500 kilometers were banned along with nuclear-armed ones because verification of warheads on individual missiles was deemed infeasible. If this precedent were applied to short-range missiles, NATO would have to forgo a promising new means of countering

* Voices on both the left and, recently, the right of the political spectrum in the Federal Republic of Germany have called for the elimination of tactical and battlefield nuclear weapons from the central region. Proponents of this third zero agreement argue that the short range of these weapons undermines the credibility of threats to employ them, since they would detonate on or near Western (read "German") territory. Other members of the Alliance, notably the United Kingdom and France, have spoken up strongly against any reductions in these weapons.

a Warsaw Pact armored offensive. (Of course, eliminating Warsaw Pact TBMs would reduce the threat to NATO assets posed by these weapons.) Likewise, most modern artillery pieces of large caliber can fire both nuclear and conventional rounds. If nuclear artillery were to be eliminated, a means would have to be found to monitor stocks of artillery ammunition—a task of enormous scope and complexity.

In summary, it is far from clear whether bilateral reductions in ground attack aircraft or tactical nuclear weapons would be in NATO's interest. And even if such reductions were judged acceptable, it is difficult to see how meaningful cuts could be implemented and effectively monitored.

How to Reduce? In addition to the question of what to reduce, the question of how to reduce will have far-reaching ramifications for the effects of an agreement on stability and security. What should constitute elimination of a piece of equipment such that it would no longer be counted against an agreed-upon ceiling?

The most obvious approach to eliminating weapons is to destroy or dismantle them. This has been the approach taken in the SALT and INF treaties: Broadly speaking, a missile or launcher is no longer counted against a treaty ceiling when it ceases to exist. Using similar dismantlement and destruction criteria in a conventional reductions regime would necessitate the cutting up or melting down of very large numbers of weapons—an approach that is both costly and quite irreversible, even if symbolically appealing to many. Since the Soviet Union could legitimately maintain a vast reserve of such weapons east of the Urals, such an approach seems risky for NATO if employed on a large scale.

This brings us to a second approach: removing the items in question from the reductions zone. Because the SALT and INF treaties are of global scope, this option was not available in those cases. But given the more narrow geographic scope of the Atlantic-to-the-Urals talks, the Soviets, the United States, and Canada will have the option of achieving compliance by moving equipment out of the region altogether, while other participants could have this option with regard to any subzones created within Europe.

This approach has disadvantages of its own, however. On its face, it would appear to favor the Soviet Union, since moving equipment the 3000 or so miles from the Urals to Central Europe remains less problematic than moving it across the Atlantic Ocean to vulnerable seaports and airports. It would also be difficult for other members of the alliances to take advantage of this provision, since (with the exception of

Denmark, which could, theoretically, use Greenland for these purposes) their own national territories lie wholly within the overall reductions zone.* Perhaps most important, however, simply removing large numbers of forces from the reductions zone as a means of complying with ceilings would allow the Soviets to redirect their existing military capabilities to other regions around their borders, with unfavorable consequences for their neighbors and for U.S. security interests in those regions.

Thus, a third approach to implementing reductions has been suggested.[23] Both sides could agree not to count equipment placed in "secured storage" against treaty ceilings, even if the storage areas were within the reductions zone. These secured storage areas would consist of fenced compounds equipped with a variety of sensors and seals to prevent the covert withdrawal of stored equipment. Compounds would be subjected to periodic and short-notice on-site inspections. The treaty would specify that equipment could be withdrawn from secured storage areas only following a notification period.

This approach seems promising for several reasons. First, it would allow any U.S. weapons in Europe that were subjected to treaty ceilings to remain in Europe. Once heavy U.S. ground forces equipment was removed from the continent (much less destroyed), it would be difficult, both logistically and, in some circumstances, politically to return it there. Secured storage would also provide countries whose entire territory lies within the reductions zone with an option less draconian than dismantlement and destruction for complying with treaty limits.

Of course, reductions implemented by consigning weapons to secured storage could be reversed if a party to the treaty chose to cease compliance *overtly*. In order to extend the period needed to break out of treaty restrictions, therefore, equipment in secured storage would need to be partially dismantled. Treads, turrets, or gun barrels could be removed from tanks and self-propelled artillery, for example. Such delaying measures would be essential in order to preclude a scenario

---

* It is not inconceivable that continental NATO nations could elect to locate some of their military equipment in the United States. Rebasing a few wings of allied aircraft in the United States, for instance, might be a particularly attractive option if the Vienna talks result in ceilings on ground attack aircraft. In a reversal of past practice, aircrews from the nation that owned the aircraft could rotate to the United States periodically for training, taking advantage of the generally superior flying weather of the American Southwest.

wherein an aggressor undertook a surprise air and missile attack on his enemy's secured storage sites while simultanously removing equipment from his own sites.

Finally, if both sides agree to impose ceilings on weapons between the Atlantic and the Urals, facilities producing these weapons within the reductions zone would have to be monitored in order to ensure continued compliance with the ceilings. Monitoring measures agreed to within the INF treaty may provide a useful model here.

How Deep Should We Cut? "How far to go?" is perhaps the single most critical question in contemplating reductions in conventional forces. Obviously, the most favorable outcome from NATO's standpoint would be simply to eliminate the very large asymmetries in key armaments—main battle tanks, artillery, infantry fighting vehicles—that currently favor the Warsaw Pact by compelling the side with more weapons to reduce to the level of the other. (As noted earlier, the Soviets claim that there are offsetting imbalances and insist that NATO must surrender its alleged advantages if Pact nations are to eliminate theirs. On the basis of an examination of publicly available data, however, we have been unable to identify any areas in which NATO has a significant numerical advantage.) A voluntary renunciation of military capabilities on such a scale would be unprecedented and barely conceivable, at least as an endpoint to the reductions process.

An outcome that resulted in common ceilings in armored vehicles and artillery at a level perhaps 10–20 percent below that of current NATO forces in the central region would seem acceptable. The resulting reductions in Warsaw Pact forces relative to NATO's would be, to borrow Secretary of State Shultz's term from Reykjavik, breathtaking. For example, if NATO were to reduce its tank and artillery forces in the central region by 15 percent and the Warsaw Pact were to bring its comparable weapons (including those deployed in the Soviet Union's three western military districts) down to that level, Pact forces would be stripped of approximately 70 percent of their tanks and artillery. The Pact would give up approximately 19,500 tanks to NATO's 1,400 (a ratio of 14:1). Likewise, the Pact's cut of 8,500 artillery pieces would be matched by 600 from NATO (again, a 14:1 ratio). Figure 14 illustrates these cuts.

Of course, by accepting heavier cuts, NATO could reduce these enormously disparate ratios. A 50 percent reduction in NATO's tanks, for example, would require a reduction of "only" 6.5 Warsaw Pact tanks for each of NATO's. But reductions by NATO of this magnitude, even if accompanied by reductions in Warsaw Pact forces to equal levels,

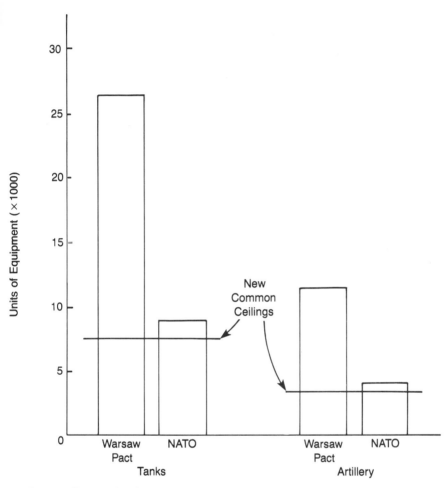

FIG. 14. *Potential Reductions in NATO and Warsaw Pact Tank and Artillery Forces in the Central Region*

would appear very risky. Put simply, it is not clear that NATO would retain sufficient forces to man fully its forward defense positions and to back these forces with the operational reserves required to cope with breakthroughs, were it reduced to such a small number of tanks and artillery.[24] In our judgment, then, such deep reductions in NATO's forces should not be contemplated unless and until evolving political military circumstances and detailed analysis of alternative military balances convince the political and military leaders of the Alliance that the residual forces would be adequate to deter aggression and prevent intimidation by the Warsaw Pact.

If Pact negotiators balk at reductions of 14:1, yet NATO cannot safely accommodate cuts in its own forces deeper than 10–20 percent, it might be best for the allies to propose, as an interim solution,[25] an outcome that resulted in something less than the full elimination of the current imbalances in these weapons. An agreement that imposed a 15 percent reduction on NATO's tank force in the central region and a 60 percent cut in the Pact's tanks, for example, would leave an imbalance of around 1.5:1 (11,000 versus 7,500 tanks)—a substantial improvement, from NATO's perspective, over today's imbalance of 3:1 (27,250 versus 9,000). Even this partial redressing of the imbalance yields a reductions ratio of approximately 10:1.

Restructuring

Radical restructuring of NATO and Warsaw Pact conventional forces has been portrayed in some quarters as something of a panacea, rendering offensive warfare infeasible. Concepts for defensive defense, which incorporate radical restructuring provisions, focus on deep cuts in armor, artillery, and ground attack aircraft on both sides, with increased emphasis on the use of mines, barriers, and short-range antitank weapons to provide defense against attack. In general, weapons that would provide a capability to conduct mobile armored ground assaults or to attack enemy forces in their rear areas are eschewed in favor of capabilities to support a strategy of defense in depth.

Remarkably, given the substantial imbalance in conventional forces in the central region currently favoring the Warsaw Pact, some Western theorists have advocated the *unilateral* restructuring of NATO's forces in order to eliminate their capabilities for offensive operations. Such an initiative, it is claimed, will convince the Soviets that the West has no intention of attacking, prompting Moscow to return the favor and begin its own military restructuring program.[26]

Some analysts in Moscow's leading foreign policy institutes have been attracted to these and similar Western ideas for nonprovocative defense. Thus, echoes of the Western proposals, sketched above, have appeared recently in official Soviet statements, including some by General Secretary Gorbachev himself, as recounted in chapter 1 and earlier in this chapter. And the final stage of the latest Soviet proposal for the new Vienna talks calls for a transition to such postures by both NATO and the Warsaw Pact.

It should be noted that virtually any agreement to reduce conventional forces on the basis of specific classes of equipment (as opposed to whole combat units) will very likely result in some restructuring of the forces to which they are applied. For example, a reduction in Warsaw Pact tanks and artillery in Central Europe to a level 15 percent below NATO's currently deployed level would result in the loss by an average Pact armored division of more than 40 percent of its total firepower, assuming the Pact retained its current number of divisions.[27] Thus, a conventional reductions agreement that truly eliminates numerical asymmetries in the forces of NATO and the Warsaw Pact might, in itself, constitute a rather fundamental restructuring of at least Warsaw Pact forces. Of course, if the Pact chose to reduce significantly the number of divisions it deployed in the wake of these equipment reductions, these restructuring effects would be diluted accordingly, although the reduction in Pact combat power within the subzone or overall area would still be realized.

If sizable portions of both sides' tanks and artillery were removed from Central Europe or were placed in secured storage hundreds of kilometers or more from the line of contact, the remaining forces would consist largely of motorized infantry forces. If these forces were well armed with modern antitank weapons and prepared to use minefields and other barriers, they might indeed possess only limited offensive capability, but be well suited to carrying out an effective defense of their own territory. Forces of this character then, closely resemble the ones that have been suggested by some advocates of "nonoffensive defense."

Given the elimination of Pact superiorities in armored forces, artillery, and perhaps other key indices of military capability, *and given a willingness on the part of NATO to give up some territory in the central region in the early phases of a war*, arms control agreements leading to the rather fundamental restructuring of NATO and Warsaw Pact forces might be acceptable. But considerable analysis of the resulting force postures would be necessary before such a step could be taken.

New Confidence- and Security-Building Measures

As noted earlier, thirty-five participants in the Stockholm II negotiations will be considering confidence- and security-building measures for Europe. A wide range of possible measures falls within the broad scope of cooperative CSBMs. These include measures to redeploy within the reductions zone selected types of weapon systems and support equipment, to constrain military exercises and other out-of-garrison activities, to require advance notification of military movements, and to provide observation opportunities that serve to increase the predictability and "transparency" of military activities. Measures to establish institutional frameworks for promoting increased under-standing, crisis avoidance, and crisis management have also been proposed. Given this lengthy menu, and given the unavoidable com-plexity of the CST negotiations, the prospects for concluding a new agreement on some of these matters in the Vienna talks on CSBMs may well be better than those for achieving force reductions under CST. Consequently, the next administration should be prepared to move quickly to develop, in concert with its allies, a concrete set of positions and proposals for the upcoming Stockholm II negotiations.

Redeployments. If reductions of the type outlined above were imple-mented by allowing some signatories (including, in particular, the Soviet Union and the United States) to move their forces out of the region of the Atlantic to the Urals rather than dismantling and destroy-ing them, this would, of course, constitute a major redeployment in itself. The basic purposes of redeployments of forces *within* the reduc-tions zone are to increase the time and logistical complications asso-ciated with initiating offensive action and to make these activities more distinctive against the background noise of other military activities.

We have already mentioned that the Soviets appear to favor the creation of a 150 kilometer wide "thin out" zone in Central Europe. The idea for selective redeployments of forces in Europe has been around for many years. A plan announced by the Polish Foreign Minister Adam Rapacki in 1957 and 1958 called for the withdrawal of all nuclear weapons from Czechoslovakia, the two Germanies, and Poland, as well as for reductions in conventional arms in that area. Subsequent Soviet-sponsored proposals in the late 1950s called for reductions by one-third or more in military forces deployed in the two Germanies.[28]

Some in the West have also called for the creation of a tank-free zone of similar dimensions. Conceivably, other items, such as self-propelled artillery, attack helicopters, mobile SAMs, and critical logistic support (such as tactical bridging equipment, mine-clearing vehicles, or major ammunition stocks) could be banned from this zone as well.

As noted earlier, a "thin out" zone that included reductions focused on selected armaments could be considered either a force reduction or a confidence-building measure. Consequently, it could be negotiated at the Conventional Stability Talks as part of a broader force reduction agreement or in the "Stockholm II" negotiations as a CSBM designed to make surprise attack more difficult.

The chief value of a rather narrow zone from which selected conven-tional weapons were eliminated would be its contribution to NATO's list of warning indicators of attack. The establishment of these zones might have no effect on the size and character of the military forces that could be brought to battle in the Central European region. And, of course, narrow exclusion or "thin-out" zones could be quickly violated by an attacker prior to war. But their existence would make the forward deployment of a significant number of forces much more visible, distinctive, and politically significant. Detection of a sizable number of tanks in the Warsaw Pact portion of a tank-free zone, for instance, would constitute a highly persuasive indication of possible preparations for an attack.

Such indications would be valuable not so much because NATO's current reconnaissance and indications and warning (I&W) capabilities are inadequate as because the political process that must act in response to the outputs of the I&W system is unpredictable. Today, it seems highly unlikely that Warsaw Pact forces could begin to mobilize without many of their activities being quickly detected by NATO. These data could support a judgment that unusual and potentially dangerous activities were under way. But NATO's military forces could not begin to increase their readiness in response without a decision by NATO's political structure to do so.

There might well be considerable discussion and delay among NATO political representatives before a decision could be made to increase NATO's readiness posture. The less ambiguous the evidence presented to the decision-makers, the more likely would be a timely NATO response to Pact mobilization. And if moving tanks and other materiel forward were a clear violation of a treaty commitment, it would remove a lot of ambiguity from this indication of mobilization activity.

Of course, violating a treaty commitment is not an action to be taken lightly, by either the transgressor or other signatories to the treaty. Thus, the advantage of a zone free of tanks or other weapons might be its drawback as well: While a tank-free zone might increase the clarity of warnings that an attack was coming, it might inhibit the defender from responding to threats of aggression, because appropriate responses would also violate the treaty. The trick, then, is to devise measures that would make preparations for offensive action more obvious without diminishing NATO's willingness to increase its own readiness levels when appropriate. One approach that has been suggested is to make such a zone 150 kilometers wide on the Warsaw Pact side and only perhaps 50 kilometers wide on NATO's.[29] Such a proposal appears reasonable, given that NATO enjoys far less depth on its side of the border than does the Pact.

Thin-out zones limiting the number of particular types of weapons within a zone but not banning them would have similar advantages and disadvantages, but such zones would be very difficult to monitor effectively. The presence of a single tank inside a tank-free zone constitutes a violation of the zone agreement. But if a ceiling of, say, 1000 were placed on the number of tanks that could be deployed in a zone, the monitoring countries would have to detect *simultaneously* at least 1001 tanks in the zone to prove a violation. Otherwise, it could be argued that weapons thought to be deployed above the ceiling had, in fact, been double-counted.

As for the notion of a nuclear weapons-free zone in Central Europe or elsewhere, it is hard to see how the creation of such a zone could strengthen NATO's security. On the contrary, moving these weapons rearward might diminish somewhat the risks that the Soviet leadership associated with a war in Europe, undermining deterrence of a Warsaw Pact attack and thus making war more likely.

Increasing Transparency and Constraining Peacetime Activities. Several steps designed primarily to verify compliance with reduction or re-deployment agreements would, if implemented, also add significantly to the transparency of both sides' military activities. For example, simply exchanging "authoritative data" and verifying its accuracy by on-site inspection—the initial steps envisaged in the Soviets' latest CST proposal—would increase the accuracy of NATO's baseline profile of Pact military deployments. Such an exchange would be really useful only if the data provided were quite detailed. Information on ground forces, for example, should cover units down to the battalion level and include each one's designation and organizational subordination, its peacetime location, its level of manning, and a listing of its equipment. Such data would be invaluable in helping analysts to detect and classify anomalous deployments or activities when they occurred. Consequently, the West should press, not only in CST but also in the Vienna talks on CSBMs, for both an initial exchange of detailed force data and periodic updates of this data base.

It might also be useful to establish procedures whereby both sides monitor on a routine basis activities at a wide range of other sites on the adversary's territory. Candidates for full-time "observation post" monitoring or short-notice inspections might include a variety of installations whose use would be associated with large-scale offensive operations, such as major ammunition and equipment storage depots, large army garrisons, key airports and seaports, and major rail lines. If coverage of such sites were sufficiently widespread, it could be impossible to mount large-scale military operations without activating a large number of observing sensors (be they human or mechanical). A less ambitious approach to serve this enhanced observation goal would be to liberalize travel restrictions on military personnel assigned to liaison missions and embassies from the Atlantic to the Urals, allowing them greater scope to travel and observe military activities.

If force reductions were implemented by placing equipment inside secured storage areas, as suggested earlier, continuous monitoring of these areas would provide a basis for warning of an impending attack, *provided the attacking side deemed it necessary to employ those assets in the opening phase of its offensive.* If, on the other hand, an attack could be commenced without removing weapons and support equipment from secured storage, leaving them undisturbed might actually create confusion in the other side's I&W assessments.

Of course, monitors can always be dismissed or disabled prior to a mobilization. But attempting to black out the monitoring network would seem to provide the most unambiguous warning possible of hostile intent.

Another approach to increased transparency would be to resurrect a version of President Eisenhower's "open skies" proposal. Ambassador Jonathan Dean has suggested that each alliance be granted a quota of approximately 100 overflights per year by reconnaissance aircraft (fixed wing and helicopter) into designated sectors of the central region.[30] Such an arrangement would significantly improve each side's ability to monitor the other's military activities.

Whatever monitoring arrangements might be agreed on, their effectiveness could be enhanced by instituting additional rules requiring advance notification of maneuvers and other out-of-garrison activities involving forces larger than an agreed-upon size. It has been suggested, for example, that ceilings be placed on the number of divisions each alliance could have out of garrison at one time.[31] Another potentially useful measure would be a ceiling on the number of reservists that could be called up for mobilization at any one time.

The United States and its allies might also consider measures that would directly restrict military reinforcement activities in Central Europe. For example, a ceiling could be placed on the maximum number of military personnel that could be introduced into Central Europe within a given period. Additionally, a CSBM regime could require advance notification of large-scale movements through designated entry and exit points. Such measures could indeed constrain the Warsaw Pact's ability to "legally" put large combat forces in the field.

Unfortunately, they might also increase the impediments to a prompt mobilization by NATO.[32]

A final type of cooperative confidence- and security-building measure would provide opportunities for senior political and military leaders from East and West to establish a continuing dialogue about national security matters, including the avoidance and management of potential crisis situations. One measure of this type would be to establish regular high-level military-to-military consultations between the opposing alliances on either a bilateral or a multilateral basis. The United States and the Soviet Union have initiated such meetings at the highest levels of their military establishments. Meetings of this type could be broadened to encompass lower-ranking officers and participants from allied nations.

Such NATO–Warsaw Pact military-to-military contacts could help build mutual understanding regarding a wide range of matters, such as the operational military doctrines of the two sides and their most serious concerns regarding each other's force developments and activities. Since 1987, the Warsaw Pact has been pressing for a meeting between the commanders in chief of the two opposing alliances in Europe and for joint discussions of military doctrines. Although the Soviets might draw on these meetings for grist in the propaganda mill, we believe that NATO should agree to such contacts on a limited, provisional basis. The senior American and Soviet officials who have participated in the U.S.–Soviet meetings have praised the benefits of learning each other's views and concerns through frank, firsthand discussions and debate.

There have also been suggestions from both East and West that a multinational crisis control center be established in Europe. This center could be jointly manned by military and diplomatic personnel drawn from the member states of NATO and the Warsaw Pact, as well as the European neutral and nonaligned states. It could play a useful role as a facility for the routine exchange of military data, for notifications of military activities, for coordinating verification and observation events, and for joint discussions of military doctrines. More important, the center could provide a supplementary communications channel and a locus for conflict resolution in the event of an actual crisis.

Summary

The Soviets' recent proclamations of their willingness to consider radical revisions in conventional force deployments in Europe justify speculation that the upcoming Vienna negotiations may provide the West with an unprecedented opportunity to redress chronic and sizable imbalances in conventional forces in Europe. Unquestionably, years of hard bargaining—within the NATO Alliance as well as between East and West—lie ahead if a useful agreement is to be hammered out. But the potential benefits of such an agreement seem well worth the effort and risks involved in its pursuit.

We share the view held by most qualified Western observers that NATO would probably be incapable of conducting a sustained conventional defense of its territory in the central region in the face of a determined Warsaw Pact invasion. The chief implications of this situation for conventional arms control are twofold:

- *NATO must insist on highly asymmetrical reductions in Warsaw Pact forces in order to offset any reductions in its own defense capabilities.* In particular, NATO must retain sufficient ground and air forces to maintain a coherent forward defense line and to provide mobile reserves to cope with breakthroughs. Reductions to equal ceilings approximately 10–15 percent below NATO's current level of forces seem safe. An outcome imposing smaller reductions and falling somewhat short of equal ceilings might also be acceptable.

- *NATO should eschew further major reductions in its theater-based nuclear forces for the time being.* These forces are needed in order to ensure that the Soviet leaders understand that war in Europe could very likely result in an outcome totally unacceptable to them. Moreover, the aircraft, missiles, and artillery pieces used to deliver these nuclear weapons play (or, in the case of missiles, shall play) important roles in NATO's conventional defense posture. It therefore would be inadvisable to accept significant reductions in these delivery systems forces, and it is infeasible to verify cuts in the nuclear warheads they carry.*

Within the context of these broad guidelines, NATO's negotiating position should embody the following basic elements:

- Reductions in conventional forces should be denominated in terms of weapons and equipment, rather than manpower, as was the case in MBFR.

---

* It may be that NATO governments will find political pressure for further reductions in theater-based nuclear forces irresistible, in which case the best approach might be to implement cuts unilaterally in nuclear artillery, while modernizing remaining forces. Enhancements should be focused on the deployment of a follow-on missile to the Lance that would have greater range and accuracy, and a standoff missile for delivery by theater-based aircraft.

- Reductions should be focused on weapons most conducive to seizing and holding territory in modern maneuver warfare: tanks, artillery, and armored personnel carriers.
- Reductions in NATO's theater-based aircraft may be acceptable if and only if the basing infrastructure needed to support them in the theater can be maintained so that rapid reinforcement is possible.
- The lion's share of reductions in ground equipment should be implemented by placing weapons in secured storage within the area from the Atlantic to the Urals. Equipment stored within these compounds must be partially dismantled in order to prevent rapid breakout.
- Assurance of compliance with a conventional force reductions agreement should be possible through an exchange of detailed data on military forces deployed between the Atlantic and the Urals, along with remote monitoring and on-site inspections of secured storage compounds, destruction and dismantlement facilities, and other key installations.
- Reductions should be accompanied by CSBMs aimed at improving the two sides' ability to monitor potential mobilization activities of each other and at reducing ambiguities in assessments of the significance of those activities.

5

Other Arms Control Initiatives

I N ADDITION TO the sets of negotiations addressed in chapters 2–4, the following areas of arms control activity are worthy of mention:

- Efforts to restrict further the testing of nuclear weapons
- Work toward a multinational treaty banning chemical weapons
- Proposals to ban the deployment of antisatellite weapons.

Although these three subjects do not, in our view, carry the same weight as those addressed earlier, they have received considerable attention, both within the U.S. government and in Soviet public diplomacy initiatives.

Nuclear Testing

Background

Early in Mikhail Gorbachev's tenure as general secretary, the Soviet Union began a vigorous campaign to push the issue of nuclear testing to the top of the arms control agenda. On July 25, 1985, twelve days before the fortieth anniversary of the U.S. bombing of Hiroshima, Mr. Gorbachev announced a unilateral moratorium on nuclear testing and called for immediate talks toward a comprehensive test ban treaty (CTBT). The moratorium was to expire on the last day of 1985 unless the United States halted its tests. Although Washington did not join in the moratorium, Moscow extended it on January 15, 1986, for three months. Still unsuccessful, the Soviets extended their testing moratorium twice more, through the end of 1986, and announced their willingness to accept unprecedented cooperative monitoring measures for verifying compliance with a test ban, declaring that they would accept whatever measures were necessary, including on-site inspections.

Even though the United States continued its nuclear weapons testing program throughout this period and beyond, the Soviet efforts to promote the idea of a test ban have met with some success. For example, it seems now to have become a yearly ritual in Washington for the House of Representatives to approve legislation calling for a one-year ban on any tests by the United States of nuclear weapons with a yield greater than one kiloton. Although this provision—usually included as an amendment to the Defense Authorization Act—is removed each year by the House-Senate conference committee, it has sent a clear signal to the White House that the testing issue cannot be ignored.

Negotiations to restrict nuclear testing involve two separate but related issues: the future status of the Threshold Test Ban Treaty and the Peaceful Nuclear Explosions Treaty (the TTBT and PNET); and the possibilities for further reductions in the permitted yield and frequency of nuclear tests, leading to an eventual comprehensive test ban (CTB).

The TTBT and PNET

The Reagan administration has consistently held that current monitoring provisions are inadequate to justify the ratification of the 1974 TTBT and the 1976 PNET, and has therefore not submitted them for ratification. The treaties would prohibit the United States and the Soviet Union from detonating nuclear weapons of a yield greater than 150 kilotons.* Each side monitors the yield of the other's nuclear weapons tests by using seismic measuring devices located outside of the national territory of the monitored states. Inherent sources of imprecision in remote seismic monitoring are magnified by the fact that each side has only imperfect knowledge of the geological conditions at the other's testing site. Specifically, experts in the United States are uncertain to what degree the rock beneath Semipalatinsk—the Soviet test site— couples, or transfers the shock of an explosion to the surrounding substrata, through which shock waves propagate to remote seismic monitors. Thus, U.S. officials judge that they may misestimate the yield of Soviet nuclear tests today by a factor of two: A 300-kiloton explosion could be assessed as between 150 and 600 kilotons.[1]

The Reagan administration has accused the Soviet Union of conducting tests of nuclear weapons whose yields were "likely" in excess of the

---

* Neither side is legally bound by the treaties until both sides have ratified them. Nevertheless, both sides have announced that they will abide by the treaties' provisions, pending ratification.

TTBT's 150-kiloton ceiling.[2] Nonetheless, the Reagan administration has stated that if both sides can agree on further measures to improve their monitoring capabilities, it would be prepared to submit the TTBT and the PNET to the Senate and to call for their ratification without reservation.

Toward that end, Secretary of State Shultz and Soviet Foreign Minister Shevardnadze signed an agreement at the Moscow summit on May 30, 1988, setting guidelines for a "joint verification experiment," in which each side will measure the yield and seismic reactions from an underground nuclear explosion at the other's test site. The two "shots" under this agreement took place in the summer of 1988. The experiment at Semipalatinsk should give American experts a much more accurate understanding of the coupling characteristics of the rock formations around the testing area, thereby providing a surer basis against which to compare future tests.

The United States has a broader goal in mind, however. It hopes that the joint verification experiment will help to convince the Soviets to accept use of an on-site monitoring mechanism called CORRTEX (for continuous reflectrometry for radius versus time experiment). The United States proposes to install CORRTEX measuring devices, which include a series of buried cables that are crushed by the shock of the detonation, at the Soviet test site each time the Soviets test a nuclear weapon with a yield in excess of 50 kilotons. Because of the lengthy preparations involved in setting up CORRTEX equipment, its routine use would reportedly require that a team of approximately thirty technicians be stationed at the Soviet test site almost continuously.

While the Soviets have not objected in principle to intrusive monitoring measures, they have stated that the approach favored by the United States will no longer be necessary following the gathering of data from the joint verification experiment in the Soviet Union. A number of American experts agree with the Soviet assertion that a series of remote seismic monitoring sites within both the United States and the Soviet Union would be sufficient for monitoring nuclear tests with acceptable accuracy once each side has better data regarding the geology around the other's test site.[3]

Toward a CTB?

Since both sides already have adopted a policy of compliance with the TTBT, ratification of the accord should have no tangible effect on either side's testing program. By contrast, a CTB would eliminate testing altogether and could thus have a significant impact on the future course of the U.S.–Soviet nuclear competition.

The United States (and, presumably, other nuclear powers as well) conducts explosive tests of nuclear weapons for four purposes:[4]

- *To support the design and development of new warheads for nuclear weapons.* In recent years, such tests have been part of the development of the Trident II (D-5) SLBM, nuclear-armed cruise missiles, and other weapons. Tests have also been devoted to the development of more exotic types of nuclear weapons, including the X-ray laser being developed under the auspices of SDIO.
- *To determine the effects of nuclear blast and radiation on U.S. weapons and support systems.* Each year, one or two U.S. nuclear weapons tests are devoted to examining how well certain military systems—satellites, nuclear warheads, electronic components—would be able to operate in the environment of a nuclear attack.
- *Basic research.* Scientists continue to use nuclear tests to explore the physics of nuclear explosions.
- *Stockpile reliability.* Periodically, the United States detonates warheads (or portions thereof) from its stockpile of nuclear weapons to ensure that they would operate as expected if used.

Stockpile reliability is the argument most prominently used by the Reagan administration in justifying its position on a CTB treaty, namely, that a comprehensive test ban is desirable as a long-term goal "when considered in the context of deep and verifiable arms reductions, improved verification capabilities, expanded confidence-building measures, and the maintenance of an effective deterrent."[5] In other words, as long as the United States and its allies rely on nuclear weapons for their security, says the Reagan administration, continued testing of nuclear weapons will be necessary in order to ensure the reliability and effectiveness of the weapons in the U.S. arsenal.

Testing the reliability of weapons actually constitutes only a minor portion of the U.S. nuclear testing program. According to press reports, the United States devotes only one or two tests per year, out of a total of approximately twenty, to this purpose.[6] And proponents of a CTB claim plausibly that such tests could be accomplished without exploding the nuclear material in a warhead, by testing instead only its nonnuclear detonator.

In our view, a CTB would affect U.S. security in three major ways. First, it would constrain but not halt the development of major new nuclear weapon systems. While it would be overly risky to develop a substantially new warhead design without testing it by explosion, designs for new delivery vehicles, such as a follow-on cruise missile or ICBM, could be based on existing warheads, of which there are a wide variety. However, development of exotic new types of nuclear weapons, such as the X-ray laser, and microwave weapons intended to disable electronic components, probably could not continue.

Proponents of a CTB implicitly assume that innovation in weapons design is likely to weaken first-strike and arms race stability. But it can also be argued that offensive weapons based on new designs can *increase* first-strike stability by allowing the deployment of more survivable retaliatory weapons.

Examples can be cited to support either contention. In fact, critics and proponents of any single weapon system can often find characteristics of that system that make its deployment either stabilizing or destabilizing, depending on how it is employed. Sea-launched cruise missiles, for example, are stabilizing because their retaliatory capability, dispersed on platforms (attack submarines and ships at sea), would be difficult for an attacker to neutralize swiftly. SLCMs can also be destabilizing, however, because they are difficult to detect both at launch and in flight. They might, therefore, lend themselves to a surprise attack on bomber bases and key C^3 nodes. In addition, they are an arms controller's nightmare because monitoring limits on their deployment is so difficult.*

Second, a CTB might marginally increase first-strike stability by leading to a gradual loss in confidence regarding the effectiveness (not the reliability) of one's nuclear weapons. The Limited Test Ban Treaty of 1963, for example, has made it difficult for the United States and the Soviet Union to acquire complete data on the effects of nuclear explosions on such targets as very hard ICBM silos, modern aircraft in flight, communications equipment, and other systems they would wish to destroy or need to rely upon during a nuclear attack. A CTB would compound the difficulties associated with refining these data. Resulting uncertainties about the vulnerability of these facilities and systems would make it marginally more difficult to plan a disarming first strike.

Finally, and perhaps most important, a CTB would contribute to the stigmatization of nuclear weapons as things to be eschewed and, if possible, disposed of. By signing a CTB, an American president could be seen as implicitly endorsing the proposition that nuclear weapons are no longer a significant factor in U.S. security strategy, that they are things of the past on which we no longer need to rely.

This last consideration surely lies behind much of the Soviets' motivation for promoting a CTB treaty. Banning the testing of nuclear weapons—first by the superpowers and later, perhaps, by other states

---

* For a more detailed discussion, see pp. 36–39.

as well—could only help accelerate movement toward a denuclearization of the East–West military balance.

Implications for Policy

Whether these three effects of a CTB—particularly the last one—are regarded, on balance, as good or bad depends largely on one's views as to the proper role of nuclear weapons in U.S. security. We believe that the West will not be able to reduce substantially its reliance on nuclear weapons and still maintain confidence in the adequacy of its military capabilities until there is firm evidence of pervasive and long-lasting change in the nature of Soviet international objectives and the East–West political and military relationship to which these have given rise. This does not mean that the West cannot, in the interim, have significantly fewer weapons or that it must continue testing weapons up to the current yield threshold of 150 kilotons. But the West ought to be very wary of agreements, initiatives, and even discussions about agreements that contribute to the stigmatization of nuclear weapons as an unworthy element of its military forces.

Washington and Moscow should by all means proceed with efforts to improve their capabilities for monitoring the yield of each other's tests, with the aim of ratifying the TTBT and the PNET. Assuming that the two sides do not agree on what constitutes an adequate monitoring capability by January 1989, the next administration ought to reexamine the question of whether CORRTEX is really necessary.

The next administration should also commission a study to examine the technical risks and benefits associated with reducing, over time, the permissible yield threshold for underground nuclear tests. But the United States would be well advised to postpone serious consideration of a CTB until tangible results of Mikhail Gorbachev's new thinking— for example, a substantial reduction or elimination of the Warsaw Pact's numerical advantages over NATO—are in hand.

Chemical Weapons

The Geneva Protocol of 1925 is the major multinational arms control measure relating to chemical weapons today. This treaty, signed by more than 100 countries, prohibits the first use of lethal or incapacitating chemical agents. It does not, however, address the issues of production, stockpiling, and retaliatory use of chemical weapons.

Negotiations toward a multilateral treaty outlawing chemical weapons (CW) altogether have been under way for approximately twenty years in Geneva, under the auspices of the United Nations

Conference on Disarmament (CD). In April 1984, the United States energized the negotiations by presenting a draft treaty that was the CW equivalent of its zero option INF treaty proposal. The U.S. proposal would ban the development, production, use, transfer, and stockpiling of chemical weapons. Most notably, the draft called for mandatory "any time, any place" on-site inspection provisions for monitoring compliance with a CW treaty.[7]

At the time, some questioned whether the American proposal was serious, since the constitutionality of such sweeping monitoring provisions was in doubt and since in the pre-Gorbachev era it seemed out of the question that the Soviet Union would ever accede to such intrusive OSI provisions.* Nonetheless, the U.S. draft treaty appears to have provided a basis for serious bargaining in Geneva, and progress toward an agreement has been accelerated somewhat by a series of bilateral U.S. and Soviet talks on chemical weapons.

The Reagan administration spurred the CW negotiations in another way as well: In 1985, after several years of trying, it secured congressional approval for funds to begin the production of new chemical weapons in the United States. These so-called "binary nerve gas weapons," which can be delivered either by aircraft or by artillery shells, are said to be safer to store and transport than existing chemical weapons because the chemicals comprising the lethal agents remain separate (and nontoxic) until the weapon is armed and fired. Production of these weapons in the United States began in December 1987.

Whether because of Washington's ambitious and comprehensive proposal in the CD, its success in reviving CW production after a long hiatus, the implementation of *glasnost* in the Soviet Union, or a combination of these factors, the Soviet Union has recently become much more candid about its own CW programs. Early in 1987, the Soviets officially acknowledged for the first time that they have deployed chemical weapons. Soon afterward, they announced that they had stopped producing them, that they had deployed no chemical weapons outside their own borders, and that they were constructing a facility for destroying chemical weapons.

The CW talks acquired added urgency around the time the United States presented its draft treaty, when chemical weapons were used in

---

* The international chemical industry is a highly competitive one. Processes used in the production of certain chemicals are closely guarded corporate secrets. Private companies in the United States and other Western countries may have the right to deny arms control inspectors access to their facilities. It is not clear whether procedures for inspecting compliance with a CW ban can be devised that would not compromise trade secrets.

the Iran–Iraq war. This development underscored not only that the international taboo on the use of lethal chemical agents had weakened, but also that the capacity to produce them had spread (or easily could spread) to many third world nations. In fact, a number of chemicals produced throughout the world as pesticides can, in highly concentrated form, also be effective as chemical weapons.

Thus, devising an effective ban on chemical weapons will be difficult: Many countries can produce them; the capability to do so is, to some extent, inherent in any modern civilian chemical industry; and corporations that operate chemical production facilities are wary of having sensitive proprietary information compromised.* In light of all this, probably the best the arms control process can do to constrain the deployment and use of chemical weapons is to prevent signatories to a CW convention from having stocks of chemical weapons in peacetime and, perhaps, from having a capability to deploy chemical weapons rapidly in wartime. This is a worthy objective that the major powers should work to achieve quickly, encouraging other nations to follow suit.

ASAT Weapons

Whether to seek a bilateral ban or limitation on ASAT weapons will be another question facing the next president.

Since the early 1970s, the Soviet Union has had a working ASAT weapon. It is known as a co-orbital ASAT because it must be carefully maneuvered to orbit close to its target and fly alongside it before attacking. It can attack satellites in low earth orbit (LEO) up to an altitude of 2000 kilometers or more.[9] Despite significant operational limitations on this system and several unilateral moratoria on ASAT testing, the Soviets are generally credited with having a reasonably effective ASAT capability.

The United States has undertaken a program to develop a more flexible ASAT weapon with altitude coverage similar to the Soviets' system. The U.S. weapon is called the miniature homing vehicle (MHV) and it is launched from an F-15 fighter aircraft. Political controversy, fiscal limitations, and technical challenges (in that order of importance) have hampered development of the MHV. The House of

---

* Nevertheless, representatives of major American chemical companies have testified before Congress that they favor a "strong, effective international treaty" banning chemical weapons. And in 1988, representatives of Canadian, European, Japanese, and U.S. chemical firms began drafting a set of recommendations relating to inspection provisions for a CW treaty.[8]

Representatives has been particularly skeptical of the need for an ASAT capability and has imposed strict funding and testing limitations on the program in recent years. The air force, beset by budgetary constraints, finally appears to have given up on the MHV, and no funds for it are included in the fiscal 1989 budget.

Both the United States and the Soviet Union have also built lasers that may have sufficient power and tracking capabilities to interfere with the operation of satellites in LEO. These lasers are not thought to represent an operational weapon, however, since they could be used only in a highly limited range of circumstances.

Despite (or perhaps in part because of) their apparent lead in ASAT capabilities, the Soviets have long sought a treaty banning the development and deployment of ASAT weapons. In the late 1970s and early 1980s, Moscow claimed that the American space shuttle would be used to interfere with Soviet satellites. And since 1985 the Soviets have pushed for a bilateral ban on "space strike weapons," which they define as weapons based in space and weapons based on the ground that can attack objects in space. (This position was motivated largely by their opposition to SDI, but it also includes both sides' ASAT systems.)

Given the apparent asymmetry between the Soviet Union and the United States in operational ASAT capabilities (and leaving aside for the moment the question of its impact on SDI), would the United States not be better off with a ban on ASATs? The answer rests on an understanding of two issues: the desirablity and the feasibility of an ASAT ban.

The Utility of ASATs

An effective ban on ASATs, assuming one could be devised, would turn space into a sanctuary where satellites of all types could be deployed without fear of attack. Some satellites pose threats to our security, while others play important stabilizing roles.[10] "Threatening" satellites include the Soviets' radar ocean reconnaissance satellite (RORSAT), which is intended to locate enemy naval forces and shipping assets in support of attacks on them. "Benign" satellites are epitomized by the satellite early warning systems (SEWS) deployed by both the United States and the Soviet Union. These networks of satellites would provide warning of launches of enemy ballistic missiles, allowing leaders to take action to ensure the survival of retaliatory assets, action that could include launching bombers, airborne command posts, and, perhaps, silo-based ICBMs. Photographic reconnaissance satellites can be stabilizing in peacetime by providing a means for monitoring force levels and compliance with arms control agreements.

They can also be destabilizing in wartime if used to assist in attacking retaliatory assets, such as mobile ICBMs or submarines at sea. The point here is simply that threatening satellites, such as RORSATs, do not deserve sanctuary. Yet each side has an interest in forswearing a capability to attack the other's stabilizing satellites, such as SEWS.

The picture is further complicated by the prospect of space-based ballistic missile defenses. Virtually any orbital BMD weapon—be it a directed-energy weapon, such as a laser or particle beam, or a kinetic-energy interceptor—could attack satellites as well as ballistic missile RVs. In fact, since satellites travel along predictable paths and are not generally surrounded by decoys, even a modestly effective space-based interceptor might be an excellent ASAT weapon, at least against low-altitude satellites. If one side or the other began to deploy BMD weapons in space, the other would be driven toward developing and deploying very capable defense-suppression capabilities (ASATs) for destroying them.

Thus, a meaningful ban on the development and deployment of ASATs would spell the end of programs to develop space-based kill mechanisms under SDI.* It would also grant the Soviets a sanctuary for their RORSAT and other threatening satellites they might devise. Ironically, then, an ASAT ban would encourage both sides to place more militarily useful capabilities—both threatening and benign—in orbit, even as it outlawed some of those capabilities.

The Feasibility of a Ban on ASATs

If a total ban on ASATs were deemed to be, on balance, desirable, could one be devised that would be effective? That is, could we be confident that, having agreed to ban ASAT weapons, the Soviet Union would lack the capability to interfere with the operation of U.S. satellites in wartime? The answer is almost certainly no.

First of all, we have no idea how many ASAT payloads the Soviets might already have constructed. Given the relatively small size and simple design of the Soviet ASAT weapon—compared with, say, an ICBM or a bomber—the Soviets could probably retain and even produce a stock of such weapons covertly and with little risk of detection, even in the presence of a highly intrusive inspection regime.

Moreover, other weapons not specifically designed as ASATs have inherent ASAT capabilities. The Soviets' Galosh exoatmospheric ABM interceptor, for instance, could be used to disable satellites in LEO by

---

* Terminating the development of such weapons would leave a large (and growing) portion of SDI's programs intact, including those relating to fixed, ground-based interceptors, and airborne and space-based sensor systems.

detonating its nuclear warhead in space. ICBMs and SLBMs have the same capability. Admittedly, employing these nuclear-armed missiles as ASATs would be rather like using a hand grenade in place of a flyswatter: Collateral damage inflicted on other satellites in the vicinity of the target could be substantial. And the political fallout associated with such attacks undertaken in peacetime or during a conventional war would be considerable. Nonetheless, such employment could not be ruled out.

So a comprehensive and effective ban on ASAT capabilities appears infeasible. Nevertheless, the United States might be better off with a partial or imperfectly verifiable ban on ASATs than without one. After all, in the testing program for their current co-orbital ASAT, the Soviets have demonstrated only a less-than-perfect capability to employ the weapon. In particular, they appear to have experienced difficulties in maneuvering the weapon close to the target and achieving the proper orientation for effective attack. Why not freeze both sides' ASAT capabilities in their present state?

Three problems beset this approach. First, a ban on further ASAT testing would not freeze Soviet ASAT capabilities. The Soviets gain valuable experience relevant to ASAT employment each time they dock a spacecraft alongside their Mir space station. The lessons learned from these maneuvers—all fully legal under the terms of an ASAT ban— could readily be applied toward improving the Soviets' ability to employ their existing ASAT effectively. It does not appear that the United States would have a comparable opportunity to perfect its nascent ASAT system legally.

Second, as repeated accusations of Soviet arms control violations from elements in the Congress and from the Reagan administration remind us, arms control agreements that cannot be well monitored invite controversy and acrimony. Thus, a poorly verifiable ban could be harmful to arms control and to the U.S.–Soviet relationship in general.

Finally, such a ban would prevent the United States from being able to neutralize threatening satellites in time of need, unless Washington were willing to undertake extreme measures, such as detonating nuclear warheads in space. The next administration will have to decide whether it is prepared to acquiesce to a Soviet capability to locate and target U.S. carrier battle groups and shipping convoys in the event of a major war.

Partial Limitations on ASATs

Several approaches that constitute partial limitations might serve U.S. security needs.

First, the United States and the Soviet Union should seize the opportunity to ban the testing and development of ASAT weapons capable of attacking satellites in orbits above LEO. Since critical SEWS and some communications satellites are deployed in these higher orbits, such a ban would be a valuable means of protecting important benign satellites.

Second, the United States should agree to a ban on ASATs based in space. Absent such a ban, both the United States and the Soviet Union might deploy "space mines," each side parking them near the other's most threatening or valuable satellites. These weapons, if deployed, could undermine both sides' security by presenting a threat to satellites that could be executed without warning, creating a potentially unstable situation in a crisis.

Agreeing to a ban on space-based ASATs would, ipso facto, entail a commitment not to develop or deploy space-based BMD systems, effectively terminating the most splashy, if not the most useful, projects under SDI. Of course, the traditional interpretation of the ABM treaty bans the development and testing of space-based BMD components already. Moreover, we presented in chapter 3 our reasons for preferring ground-based over space-based BMD interceptors and for adhering to the traditional interpretation of the ABM treaty. In our view, forgoing the development of space-based ASATs would have no ill effects on future U.S. BMD options.

If the United States and the Soviet Union (and, conceivably, other nations with assets in orbit as well) were unable to agree to ban space-based BMD weapons, they might consider defining "keep out" zones for various orbital altitudes and locations. Such an agreement would permit specific groups of countries (Western, East bloc, and Third World), to deploy satellites only in certain zones.[11] Satellites that entered a sector not assigned to them could be destroyed. Exceptions could be permitted if the nation owning the satellite presented it for inspection prior to launch.

Third, it seems clear that, for better or worse, the clock cannot be turned back to a time when satellites in LEO were invulnerable to attack. Accordingly, the United States will have to devote further resources to increasing the survivability of its satellites in LEO that are to perform critical wartime missions. Survivability can be substantially enhanced through combinations of improved hardening, shielding, maneuverability, signature reduction (or stealth), jamming capability, and proliferation of satellites.

Additionally, the United States ought to have some capability to threaten Soviet satellites in LEO. An ideal U.S. ASAT would have the capability both to destroy threatening satellites and to offer a measure of protection to U.S. satellites by having a capability to attack the Soviets' co-orbital ASAT before it could engage a U.S. satellite. That is, a U.S. ASAT should serve as an anti-ASAT as well.

6

Future Paths

FROM THEIR BEGINNINGS, relations between the United States and the Soviet Union have been characterized by a series of oscillations between hostility and suspicion on the one hand and excessively optimistic expectations on the other. American participation in the effort to overturn the Bolshevik regime during the closing days of World War I and the Red Scare of the 1920s gave way in 1933 to a brief period of euphoria in the United States following President Roosevelt's decision to grant diplomatic recognition to the Soviet government. Soon thereafter, however, disillusionment set in among most Americans as disputes arose about the repayment of Russian debts to America and as Stalin conducted his first series of purge trials. By the end of 1941, all was forgiven, and lend-lease aid flowed to the Soviet Union as Hitler's armies rolled toward Moscow.

Washington had hoped that the patterns of Great Power cooperation forged during the Second World War would carry over into the postwar world. But Stalin's consolidation of the Soviet glacis in Eastern Europe, followed by the Korean War in 1950, drove U.S.–Soviet hostilities to their highest levels ever. Brief periods of détente in the late 1950s, 1967, and 1972–1975 could not withstand clashes over the downing of the American U-2 reconnaissance plane, the status of Berlin, fighting in Southeast Asia, the brutal crushing of a liberalizing government in Czechoslovakia, steadily growing Soviet military capabilities, and a series of Soviet gains in the Third World.

Now, in the late 1980s, the two superpowers are entering another period in which cooperation and optimism dominate hostility. The American president who once described Moscow as the focus of evil in

142

the world met with the Soviet leader four times in less than three years. In the days following the Moscow summit of 1988, President Reagan spoke expansively of hope for "a new era in human history" that had been kindled by the process of reform and détente initiated by General Secretary Gorbachev.[1]

The 1990s may witness yet another swing of the pendulum back toward hostility and distrust between East and West, in which case neither side will likely be prepared to give up significant military capabilities. Alternatively, the major powers might be able to break the historical pattern of oscillation in East–West relations and continue along a path of increasing cooperation. Because Mr. Gorbachev has, at least rhetorically, so unambiguously repudiated the policies of his predecessors and, more important, because he is pressing for democratizing reforms in the Soviet Communist Party and government, one is tempted to conclude that the latest period of East–West detente may have considerably greater staying power than earlier ones.

The Soviet leader's readiness to consider creative solutions to long-standing military problems—most notably, his acceptance of intrusive inspections for monitoring limits on military activities and weapons—augurs well for the future. And the Soviet Union's ongoing withdrawal of forces from Afghanistan, coupled with its support for efforts to pressure its client states, Angola and Vietnam, to resolve festering regional conflicts, provides evidence that Moscow is prepared, at least for the time being, to rely less upon direct military means to compete with the United States for influence in the Third World.

Arms control will always be more a *result* of political détente than a *cause* thereof. While arms control agreements can provide important incentives to adhere to informal "rules of the road" in the conduct of foreign and defense policy, the conclusion of such agreements and compliance with them cannot rule out serious clashes of interest between the superpowers. For arms control is, as we have noted, largely an ancillary tool of security policy. Only rarely are great powers willing to consign decisively important elements of their own security to a treaty framework. Rather, they most often choose to retain unilateral control over the major levers of power, sometimes viewing arms control as a means to facilitate and supplement these unilateral measures.

Nonetheless, arms control can play an important role in the evolution of East–West security relations during the 1990s. If the process of détente inaugurated by Mikhail Gorbachev's new approaches to international security gathers momentum, distrust and suspicions on both sides may begin increasingly to give way to perceptions of common security interests. Thus far, the Soviet leader's new political thinking in the sphere of international security policy has been manifested mainly in words. The major concrete result of Mr. Gorbachev's international security policy to date—the INF treaty—arguably serves the Soviet Union's interests whether or not Moscow intends to alter its traditional political-military objectives. The clearest way for Moscow to demonstrate its commitment to a cooperative approach to security is to begin dismantling its numerically superior conventional forces in Europe.

Should the Soviets begin this process in earnest, détente would quickly gain momentum as the West reexamined the continued utility of its own large-scale military deployments that originated during periods of heightened tension. Arms control can be the midwife of major adjustments in the military forces of both sides, facilitating the transition to a military balance characterized by far lower levels of forces. And the successful implementation of arms control agreements would itself lend further momentum to the process of disengagement and demobilization.

Such an outcome would fall short of ushering in the millennium, at least within the lifetimes of these youngish authors. Even in the rosiest of scenarios, capable military forces, including sizable numbers of nuclear weapons, would continue to be needed to protect fundamental national values from the atavistic, aggressive impulses of others. But should the broader political climate continue to improve, a wide range of arms control agreements could be concluded, allowing the United States, the Soviet Union, and their allies to maintain stability and security at far lower levels of forces, while diverting enormous amounts of resources to other pressing concerns.

Glossary of Acronyms and Abbreviations

ABM—anti-ballistic missile
ACM—advanced cruise missile
ADM—atomic demolition mine
ALCM—air-launched cruise missile
ALPS—accidental launch protection system
ASAT—anti-satellite weapon
ASW—anti-submarine warfare
ATACMS—army tactical missile system
ATGW—anti-tank guided weapon
BMD—ballistic missile defense
C^3—command and control communications
CD—The (United Nations') Conference on Disarmament
CDE—Conference on Disarmament in Europe
CORRTEX—"Continuous reflectrometry for radius versus time experiment" (a means for estimating the yield of underground nuclear explosions)
CSBM—confidence and security-building measures
CSCE—Conference on Security and Cooperation in Europe
CST—Conventional Stability Talks
CTBT—Comprehensive (nuclear) Test Ban Treaty
CW—chemical weapons
FBIS—The Foreign Broadcast Information Service
FRG—The Federal Republic of Germany
FROD—functionally related observable difference
HML—hardened mobile launcher
ICBM—intercontinental ballistic missile
INF—intermediate nuclear forces–nuclear delivery means with ranges between 300 and 3400 nautical miles
I & W—indications and warning
JTACMS—joint tactical missile system

LEO—low-earth orbit

LUA—launch under attack

MAD—mutual assured destruction

MBFR—Mutual and Balanced Force Reductions (negotiations)

MHV—miniature homing vehicle (a U.S. ASAT weapon)

MIRV—multiple, independently-targetable reentry vehicle

MM—"Minuteman" The name given to the class of solid-fuel ICBMs deployed in the 1960s and 1970s e.g., MMII, MMIII.

MPS—multiple protection shelters

MRL—multiple rocket launcher

MX—"Missile-experimental" The development name given to the 10-RV ICBM deployed by the United States in the 1980s. Although the Reagan administration has renamed it "Peacekeeper" the name MX seems to have stuck.

NATO—North Atlantic Treaty Organization

NTM—national technical means (refers to surveillance systems used to verify compliance with arms control treaties)

OSI—on-site inspection

PNET—peaceful nuclear explosions treaty

RORSAT—radar ocean reconnaissance satellite

RV—reentry vehicle (on a ballistic missile, a warhead or a heavy decoy meant to simulate a warhead)

SAC—The U.S. Strategic Air Command

SALT—Strategic Arms Limitations Talks

SAM—surface-to-air missile

SCC—Standing Consultative Commission

SDI—The Strategic Defense Initiative

SDIO—Strategic Defense Initiative Organization

SEWS—satellite early warning system (a space-based system for detecting enemy ballistic missile launchers)

SICBM—small ICBM (also known as the "Midgetman." This is the name given to the 40,000 lb. class-ICBM under development by the United States.)

SLBM—submarine-launched ballistic missile

SLCM—sea-launched cruise missile

SNDV—strategic nuclear delivery vehicle

SRAM—short-range air-to-surface missile

SSBN—The designation given to U.S. nuclear-powered submarines that carry SLBMs.

SSN—The designation given to U.S. nuclear-powered attack submarines.

START—Strategic Arms Reductions Talks

TBM—tactical ballistic missile

TTBT—Threshold (nuclear) Test Ban Treaty

USSR—Union of Soviet Socialist Republics (Soviet Union)

APPENDIX

START-Constrained Forces (Estimated)
(mid-1990s)

	United States				Soviet Union			
	Force	#	TWt. (x 1000 kg)	Weapons	Force	#	TWt. (x 1000 kg)	Weapons
ICBM	PK (silo)	50	180	500	SS-18 (FO) (silo)	154	1232	1540
	MMIII (silo)	152	167	456	SS-24 (rail)	112	336	1120
	PK (rail)	48	173	480	SS-25 (mobile)	344	241	344
	or	or	or			610	1809	3004
	SICBM (mobile)	480	336					
		250–682	520–683	1436				
SLBM	D-5 (17 Tri) (8 RV)	408	816	3264	SS-N-20 (5 Typhoon)	100	210	1000
					SS-N-23 (14 D IV)	224	448	896
					(19 subs)	324	658	1896
Bomber	B-52 (ALCM)	84	—	1008	Bear H (ALCM)	75	—	900
	B-52	60	—	"60"/480	Blackjack	200	—	"200"/3200
	B-1B	100	—	"100"/1600		275	—	"1100"/4100
	B-2	132	—	"132"/1584				
		376	—	"1300"/4672				
	Totals	1034–1466	1336–1499	"6000"/9372	*Totals*	1209	2467	"6000"/9000

147

Notes

Notes to Chapter 1

1. Igor Malashenko, "Parity Reassessed," *New Times*, No. 47/87, November 1987, pp. 9–10; Andrei Kortunov, researcher at the USSR's Institute for the Study of the United States and Canada, private conversation with the author, Washington, D.C., January 1988.
2. Cf. Marshal S. L. Sokolov, "In Defense of Peace and the Security of the Motherland," *Pravda*, February 23, 1987; Marshal S. F. Akhromeyev, "The Glory and Pride of the Soviet People," *Sovetskaya Rossiya*, February 21, 1987; and Army General D. T. Yazov, "The Military Doctrine of the Warsaw Pact: A Doctrine of the Defense of Peace and Socialism," *Pravda*, July 27, 1987.
3. Yazov, "Military Doctrine."
4. Colonel General N. Chervov, chief of the Treaty and Legal Directorate of the Soviet General Staff, private conversation with the author, New York, July 1988.
5. Stephen M. Meyer, "The Impact of Gorbachev's New Political Thinking on Soviet Military Programs and Operations," statement before the Defense Policy Panel of the House Armed Services Committee, Washington, D.C., July 14, 1988.

Notes to Chapter 2

1. "Mobile ICBMs: The Difficult Task of Verification," *Arms Control Update*, No. 7, July 1988, p. 5.
2. "Joint Document: 'Realistic Approach' to Reducing Nuclear Risk," *New York Times*, June 2, 1988, p. A17.
3. See Sam Nunn, "Our Allies Have to Do More," *New York Times*, July 10, 1988, section 4, p. 31.
4. See, for example, Richard L. Garwin, "Reducing Dependence on Nuclear Weapons: A Second Nuclear Regime," in David C. Gompert et al., *Nuclear*

149

Weapons and World Politics, McGraw-Hill, New York, 1977, p. 126; Marshal S. Akhromeyev, "Naval Forces and Universal Security," *Pravda*, September 5, 1988, p. 6; and V. Kalugin, "On the Seas and Oceans: The Naval Aspects of Security," *Pravda*, April 28, 1988.

5. See Michael Brower, "Why the B-2 Will Bomb: The Problems Stealth Can't Hide," *Arms Control Today*, Vol. 18, No. 7, September 1988, p. 22.

6. See Congressional Budget Office, *The B-1B Bomber and Options for Enhancements*, Washington, D.C., August 1988, pp. 63–74.

7. Congressional Budget Office, *Modernizing U.S. Strategic Offensive Forces: Costs, Effects, and Alternatives*, Washington, D.C., 1987, p. 85.

8. See Desmond Ball, *Targeting for Strategic Deterrence*, IISS Adelphi Paper No. 185, International Institute of Strategic Studies, London, Summer 1983, pp. 26–32. See also Michael M. May, George F. Bing, and John D. Steinbruner, "Strategic Arms Reductions," UCRL Preprint No. 96886, Lawrence Livermore Laboratory, June 30, 1987.

9. United Nations, *Demographic Yearbook, 1985*, The United Nations, New York, 1986, pp. 279–282.

Notes to Chapter 3

1. Harold Brown, "We're Off to a Good START," *Washington Post*, December 13, 1987, p. M2.

2. "What if a free people could live secure in the knowledge that their security did not rest upon the threat of instant U.S. retaliation to deter a Soviet attack, that we could intercept and destroy strategic ballistic missiles before they reached our soil . . . ? Isn't it worth every investment necessary to free the world from the threat of nuclear war?" *Weekly Compilation of Presidential Documents*, March 23, 1983, pp. 447–448.

3. One recent study concluded that the cost ratio would likely favor the offense by more than 4:1. For a summary, see "The Cost-Effectiveness of Strategic Defense," in *National Defense Research Institute Annual Report, Contract Year 1987*, The RAND Corporation, Santa Monica, 1988, pp. 46–48. For a thorough evaluation of the likely effectiveness of a wide range of candidate ABM technologies, as well as the most important potential countermeasures to them, see Harold Brown, "Is SDI Technically Feasible?" *Foreign Affairs*, Vol. 64, No. 3, 1986, pp. 435–454; see also James R. Schlesinger, "Rhetoric and Realities in the Star Wars Debate," *International Security*, Summer 1985, pp. 3–12. For a thorough analysis of possible operational as well as technical countermeasures available to the Soviet Union, see Stephen M. Meyer, "Soviet Strategic Programmes and the U.S. SDI," *Survival*, November/December 1985, pp. 274–292; see also Kevin N. Lewis, *Possible Soviet Responses to the Strategic Defense Initiative: A Functionally Organized Taxonomy*, The RAND Corporation, Santa Monica, N-2478-AF, July 1986.

4. See Anne H. Cahn, Martha C. Little, and Stephen Daggett, "Nunn and Contractors Sell ALPS," *Bulletin of the Atomic Scientists*, June 1988, pp. 10–12.

Notes to Chapter 4

1. Bureau of Public Affairs, United States Department of State, "Special Report No. 176," Washington, D.C., February 15, 1988, p. 4.
2. John Borawski, Stan Weeks, and Charlotte E. Thompson, "The Stockholm Agreement of September 1986," *Orbis*, Winter 1987, pp. 643–662; and John Borawski, "Accord at Stockholm," *Bulletin of the Atomic Scientists*, December 1986, pp. 34–36.
3. Ellen Jones, *Red Army and Society: A Sociology of the Soviet Military*, Allen and Unwin, Boston, 1985, pp. 52–58.
4. Edmund Brunner, Jr., *Soviet Demographic Trends and the Ethnic Composition of Draft Age Males, 1980–1995*, N-1654-NA, RAND Corporation, Santa Monica, February 1981, pp. 17–24.
5. For a discussion of this perspective, see John Van Oudenaren, *Soviet Policy Toward Western Europe—Objectives, Instruments, Results*, R-3310-AF, RAND Corporation, Santa Monica, February 1986, pp. 1–9.
6. For a review of the evolution of Eastern and Western positions in the MBFR talks that have been under way since 1973, see Jonathan Dean, *Watershed in Europe: Dismantling the East–West Confrontation*, Lexington Books, Lexington MA., 1987, pp. 153–184.
7. See Mr. Gorbachev's address to the East German party congress, *FBIS Daily Report, Soviet Union*, April 18, 1986, p. F8.
8. The Budapest Appeal was signed by the Warsaw Pact nation party chiefs on June 11, 1986. See *FBIS Daily Report, Soviet Union*, June 13, 1986, pp. B8–12.
9. Mr. Gorbachev first proposed this asymmetrical reductions approach when he addressed a special "peace forum" that had been convened in Moscow in February 1987 to publicize the Soviet Union's new political thinking on national security policy and arms control. See "Gorbachev Addresses Forum," *FBIS Daily Report, Soviet Union*, February 17, 1987, pp. AA15–26.
10. See Paul Lewis, "Soviet Offers to Adjust Imbalance of Conventional Forces in Europe," *New York Times*, June 24, 1988, pp. A1–A2.
11. *Documents of the Meeting of the Political Consultative Committee of the Warsaw Treaty Member States, Warsaw, July 15–16, 1988*, Novosti Press Agency Publishing House, Moscow, 1988.
12. Ibid.
13. "Gorbachev's 28 July speech in Vladivostok," *FBIS Daily Report, Soviet Union*, July 29, 1987, pp. R16–19; "Gorbachev Speaks to [Indian] Parliament," *FBIS Daily Report, Soviet Union*, November 28, 1986, pp. D6–12; and "Gorbachev Interviewed by Indonesian Paper *Merdeka*," *FBIS Daily Report, Soviet Union*, July 23, 1987, pp. C1–10.
14. U.S. Department of State, "Arms Control: Progress and Global Challenges," *Current Policy*, No. 1080, June 13, 1988, p. 2.
15. Ibid.
16. Interview with General John Galvin, *Defense News*, August 1, 1988, p. 30.
17. Interview with General Bernard Rogers, *Newsweek*, April 27, 1987, p. 27.

18. Quoted by Stanley Kober in "The Trouble with Conventional Defense," *Washington Post*, July 11, 1988, p. A11.

19. See James A. Thomson and Nanette C. Gantz, *Conventional Arms Control Revisited: Objectives in the New Phase*, N-2697-AF, RAND Corporation, Santa Monica, December 1987.

20. See Joshua M. Epstein, "Dynamic Analysis and the Conventional Balance in Europe," *International Security*, Vol. 12, No. 4, Spring 1988, pp. 154–165. For assessments by other civilian academic specialists who are sanguine about NATO's ability to hold in the face of massive Warsaw Pact attacks, see John Mearsheimer, "Why the Soviets Can't Win Quickly in Central Europe," *International Security*, Vol. 12, No. 4, Spring 1988, pp. 174–185; and Barry Posen, "Is NATO Decisively Outnumbered?," *International Security*, Vol. 12, No. 4, Spring 1988, pp. 186–202. For a detailed critique of these views, see Eliot A. Cohen, "Toward Better Net Assessment," *International Security*, Vol. 13, No. 1, Summer 1988, pp. 50–89.

21. Figures by Philip Karber; cited in Anthony H. Cordesman, "Fatal Flaws in Presenting the NATO/Warsaw Pact Balance," *Armed Forces Journal*, July 1988, p. 60. Karber's tank balance figures, for example, are 6,970 for NATO versus 16,950 for the Warsaw Pact; in contrast, the IISS cites figures of 12,700 versus 18,000 (*Military Balance 1987–88*). (Note that the MBFR guidelines area is smaller than the region for which forces are depicted in Figures 14 and 15. Most notably, the guidelines area omits the western military districts of the Soviet Union).

22. By all indications, the NATO countries have adopted this basic approach. For a more detailed treatment of this and other approaches, see Robert D. Blackwill and James A. Thomson, "A Countdown for Conventional Arms Control," *Los Angeles Times*, October 25, 1987, Outlook section, pp. 1, 2, and 6.

23. See Jonathan Dean, "The New NATO-Pact Force Reductions Talks—An Optimal Outcome," paper prepared for the American Academy of Arts and Sciences, Washington, D.C., May 18, 1988, pp. 16–17.

24. For a fuller exploration of this subject, see James A. Thomson and Nanette C. Gantz, *Conventional Arms Control Revisited: Objectives in the New Phase*, N-2697-AF, RAND Corporation, Santa Monica, December 1987, pp. 6–12.

25. "Interim solution" is proposed here as a term of art that would allow NATO to avoid the appearance of accepting, as a matter of principle, a continuing (albeit greatly reduced) Warsaw Pact superiority in armor and artillery in the central region.

26. See, for example, Andreas von Buelow, "Defensive Entanglement: An Alternative Strategy for NATO," in Andrew J. Pierre, ed., *The Conventional Defense of Europe: New Technologies and New Strategies*, Council on Foreign Relations, New York, 1986, pp. 112–151.

27. For a listing of equipment types in NATO and Warsaw Pact divisions, and the contribution of each type to a division's firepower, see William P. Mako, *U.S. Ground Forces and the Defense of Central Europe*, The Brookings Institution, Washington, D.C., 1983, Appendix A, pp. 105–125.

28. See U.S. Department of State, *Documents of Disarmament, 1945–1959,* Vol. II, Washington, D.C., August 1960, pp. 607, 754, 892, 1032, and 1217–1218.

29. See Dean, "NATO-Pact Force Reduction Talks."

30. Ibid, p. 11.

31. John Borawski, "Practical Steps for Building Confidence in Europe," *Arms Control Today,* March 1988, pp. 17–18.

32. For a comprehensive review of options for CSBMs, see Stanley Sloan and Mikaela Sawtelle, *Confidence Building Measures and Force Constraints for Stabilizing East–West Military Relations in Europe,* Congressional Research Service Publication No. 88-591F, Washington, D.C., 1988. See also remarks by Senator Timothy Wirth in Committee on Armed Services, United States Senate, "National Defense Authorization Act for Fiscal Year 1989," Report 100-326, May 4, 1988, pp. 190–193.

Notes to Chapter 5

1. Remarks of an unidentified Defense Department official quoted in *Aerospace Daily,* August 5, 1988, p. 197.

2. United States Department of State, *Nuclear Testing Limitations: U.S. Policy and the Joint Verification Experiment,* Washington, D.C., 1988, p. 2. This finding has been disputed by a wide range of American scientists. A review conducted in May 1988 by the congressional Office of Technology Assessment concluded that the available evidence could not prove that the Soviet Union had not complied with the TTBT. See R. Jeffrey Smith, "Soviet Team to Monitor H-Bomb Test," *Washington Post,* August 16, 1988, p. A4.

3. See Sandra Blakeslee, "Soviets Prepare for Verification at Nevada Site," *New York Times,* August 15, 1988, p. A1.

4. See William J. Broad, "U.S. Is Committed to Nuclear Tests," *New York Times,* October 18, 1987, p. 1.

5. *Arms Control Issues,* United States Arms Control and Disarmament Agency, Washington, D.C., February 8, 1985, p. II-G–1.

6. Broad, "U.S. Is Committed to Nuclear Tests."

7. United States Department of State, *U.S. Arms Control Initiatives,* Special Report No. 177, Washington, D.C., May 13, 1988, p. 3.

8. See "The U.S. Inventory," *Newsweek,* August 22, 1988, p. 49.

9. United States Department of Defense, *Soviet Military Power,* fourth edition, Washington, D.C., 1985, pp. 55–56.

10. This analysis owes much to an excellent review of ASAT capabilities and arms control options by Ashton B. Carter, "Satellites and Anti-Satellites—The Limits of the Possible," *International Security,* Spring 1986, pp. 46–98.

11. See Brian Chow, *An Agreement on Self-Defense Zones in Space,* R&D Associates, Marina del Rey, CA, 1985.

Note to Chapter 6

1. "Excerpts from President Reagan's Address on U.S.–Soviet Relations," *New York Times,* June 4, 1988, p. 6.

Index

Accidental launch protection system (ALPS), 76, 80
"Accountable weapons" under START, 23–24
Advanced cruise missiles (ACMs), 43, 45. *See also* Cruise missiles
Afghanistan, 2, 143
Aircraft (conventional force), 110, 112, 113, 114, 199; helicopters, 107–109, 110, 122. *See also* Bombers
Air defense (strategic), 69, 73
Air-launched cruise missiles (ALCMs), 23, 29–30, 35–36, 41, 43, 45, 64. *See also* Cruise missiles
Antiballistic Missile (ABM) treaty, 2, 18, 23, 27, 32; accidental launch protection system (ALPS) and, 76, 80; ASAT weapons and, 71, 85, 87; BMD policy options and, 79–85; competitive BMD deployment and, 77, 78; cooperative transition option and, 78, 79; crisis (first-strike) stability and, 67–69, 74, 76, 77, 80; economic benefits of, 5–6; next administra-

tion (after 1989) and, 73–97; next administration's (after 1989) interpretation of, 85–88; point defenses option and, 76–77; Reagan administration and, 11, 66, 70, 71, 73; SDI and, 66, 70, 71, 72–73, 85, 86, 87, 88; START and, 66, 67, 72; strategic defense and, 67–69; testing in space and, 72; U.S. and Soviet positions (since 1983) and, 70–73
Antisatellite (ASAT) weapons, 71, 85, 87, 136–41
Antisubmarine warfare (ASW), 42–43, 48. *See also* Submarines
Armored forces (conventional arms control), 110, 118–19, 121, 122, 123, 124
Arms control: Gorbachev and, 12–16, 143; military balance and, 1–2; national security (Soviet and U.S.), and 3–8; operational measures and, 2, 3; Reagan and, 8–11, 143; Soviet–U.S. relations in past and future and, 142–44; structural measures and, 2, 3; U.S.

155

Council on Foreign Relations Study Group on The Arms Control Agenda for the Next Administration

Participants

Harold Brown, Chairman, Johns Hopkins Foreign Policy Institute
Michael Mandelbaum, Group Director, Council on Foreign Relations
Cynthia B. Paddock, *rapporteur*, Council on Foreign Relations

Coit D. Blacker, author, Stanford University
Joshua Epstein, author, Brookings Institution
Arnold Kanter, author, Rand Corporation
David Ochmanek, author, Rand Corporation
R. Jeffery Smith, author, *The Washington Post*

Les Aspin, U.S. House of Representatives
Maj. Gen. George Lee Butler USAF, Joint Chiefs of Staff
Antonia Handler Chayes, ENDISPUTE, Inc.
James W. Davis, Jr., Council on Foreign Relations
Alton Frye, Council on Foreign Relations
Frank Gaffney, American Enterprise Institute
Arthur Hartman, Johns Hopkins University
Brian Hehir, Department of Social Development & World Peace
Spurgeon Keeny, The Arms Control Association
Joseph Kruzel, Ohio State University
Stanley Kwieciak, U.S. Army, Visiting Military Fellow
Jan Lodal, Intelus
Paul H. Nitze, Special Advisor to the President
Alan Platt, Rand Corporation
Karen Puschel, International Affairs Fellow in residence
Brent Scowcroft, Kissinger Associates
Stephen Sestanovich, Center for Strategic and International Studies
Walter B. Slocombe, Caplin & Drysdale, Chartered
John Steinbruner, Brookings Institution
Strobe Talbott, *Time* Inc.
Edward L. Warner, Rand Corporation
R. James Woolsey, Shea & Gardner

About the Authors

Dr. Edward Warner is a senior defense analyst at the RAND Corporation office in Washington, D.C. He conducts studies on Soviet defense and foreign policy, contemporary arms control issues, and American military policy. A former Air Force officer, his 20 years of service included: an assignment as an intelligence officer with the 93rd Bomb Wing (SAC), Castle AFB, California; teaching political science at the U.S. Air Force Academy; a tour as an analyst of Soviet defense matters with the CIA; duty as an Assistant Air Attache in the U.S. Embassy in Moscow, and work as a special assistant to General Lew Allen, the U.S. Air Force Chief of Staff. Dr. Warner is a graduate of the U.S. Naval Academy and received his masters and doctorate degrees in politics from Princeton University. Dr. Warner is adjunct professor teaching graduate seminars on Soviet military policy at both George Washington University and the Harriman Institute at Columbia University.

David Ochmanek is a defense analyst with the RAND Corporation. He specializes in issues relating to strategic forces, arms control, and tactical air forces. Prior to joining Rand he was a Foreign Service Officer, serving in Washington as a political-military policy analyst at the Department of State and in the Federal Republic of Germany. He has also served as an intelligence officer in the United States Air Force. Mr. Ochmanek is a graduate of the United States Air Force Academy and the Woodrow Wilson School of Public and International Affairs at Princeton University.